The
RHYTHM
of Discipleship

living as fully devoted followers of Christ

TRENT CASTO

with Verla Wallace

D1501687

For the people at Covenant Church—
past, present, and future

Your legacy of passion
and commitment to the gospel
inspires me

*All authority in heaven and on earth
has been given to me. Go therefore
and make disciples of all nations,
baptizing them in the name of the Father
and of the Son and of the Holy Spirit,
teaching them to observe all that I have
commanded you. And behold, I am with you
always, to the end of the age.*

Matthew 28:18–20

CONTENTS

ACKNOWLEDGMENTS

The thoughts and ideas presented in this book have been developed over many years through the influence of more people than I can count. But I would like to extend special thanks to the loving family at Covenant Church who inspired the messages which form the backbone of this book, to the elders of Covenant who have encouraged me to lead towards discipleship, and to the staff and lay leaders at Covenant who are working to create an environment for the concepts in this book to come to life.

Special thanks also to Pastor Todd Augustine for his valued contribution in the spiritual gifts section, to Marsha Phillips for her excellent work on the book cover design, and to Verla Wallace who worked tirelessly over many months to bring clarity and freshness to every single page and kept us moving all the way to the finish line.

Finally, a heartfelt thanks to my wife Emily, and children Hudson, Anna Katherine, and William, who love me at my worst and live the Rhythm with me year after year.

INTRODUCTION

Social anthropologists say the best way to get to know a people group is to study their values and how they live and act with each other and the world around them.

At Covenant, we want you to know as much as possible about *us*—and as soon as possible—so you can more quickly feel at home in the "people group" that is Covenant Church.

Here's a good place to start:

Our Vision
A loving family, dependent on the Holy Spirit,
committed to the Word, growing in grace,
reaching out in mercy.

Our Mission
We will develop and deploy fully devoted
followers of Jesus Christ
to disciple our family, community, and world.

We work hard to translate those words into real-life behavior and action. As Ruth Haley Barton says in her book *Sacred Rhythms*, discipleship doesn't happen by accident.

> Living into what we want in any area of our life requires some sort of intentional approach. Building a solid financial base, retirement planning, home improvements,

career advancement, further education, losing weight or becoming more fit—all of these require a plan if we are to make any progress in achieving what we desire. The desire for a way of life that creates space for God's transforming work is no different.

As a church, we've developed our own intentional plan, a rhythm, for living out our vision and mission day in and day out. It's a gospel-centered pattern of behaviors and practices that we believe will help us become a loving family of fully devoted followers of Christ.

It's built around four core discipleship principles we call our Rhythm of Discipleship:

- **Worship**
- **Grow**
- **Serve**
- **Go**

In this book, I'll unpack these four principles in more detail, with a valuable contribution from our Assistant Pastor Todd Augustine.

I hope you'll take the time to let these principles take deep root in your heart. Ask God for help with those parts that may be new to you or outside your comfort zone right now. And ask him what he wants you to do with what you've read.

We're all pilgrims on a journey, at different places along the way. Join us! Let's take the journey together.

Trent Casto, Senior Pastor
Covenant Church of Naples
Naples, Florida
January 2018

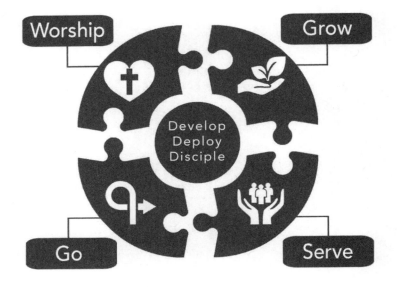

Chapter 1

THE RHYTHM

OF

DISCIPLESHIP

We live in a world of bad news. In the past year alone our nation endured multiple catastrophic hurricanes, the largest mass shooting in modern U.S. history, and wildfires that, in less than a year, have burned two million acres—an area the size of Rhode Island and Delaware combined. There are threats of nuclear war outside our borders and child sex trafficking in our own backyard.

Stories of corporate corruption reveal another company that has placed profit above ethics. Stories of mud-slinging politicians never end, while, stories go unwritten about veterans and unborn children who are dying at alarming rates. It's a 24/7 assault on our senses.

Into this bad news comes the church with her utterly unique mission: to bring the light of Christ into this dark world.

This massive mobilization effort—which we call The Great Commission—was first launched in Matthew 28:18-20, when Christ called his own disciples to spread the good news of the gospel. The gospel was God's remarkable plan to redeem humanity from the consequences of sin that had severed our relationship with a holy God. God wanted his kids back and Christ would make a way, through his death on the cross, for us to be reconciled to God through faith in Jesus Christ.

Today, God's mobilization effort continues with us.

We're called to bring good news
to people living in the midst of bad news.

The Great Commission and the gospel are at the core of our faith and the basis of our own Mission Statement: We will develop and deploy fully devoted followers of Jesus Christ to disciple our family, community, and world.

We say it often at Covenant. It's easy to recite. But what does it look like to *live* it day in and day out? In the pages that follow we'll talk about how to do it. But, first, let's talk about the *why* and *what* of our Mission Statement.

* * *

The "Why" of our Mission

Are we supposed to make disciples just because Jesus thought it would give us something to do until he returns? No. It's much bigger than that.

We pursue our mission because the gospel is *really* good news.

It's good news because God gave Jesus complete authority over everything in heaven and on earth, the entirety of the universe in which we're called to live and serve. (Matthew 28:18, Ephesians 1:20-21)

It means Jesus possesses the power (the ability) and the authority (the right) to do with the universe whatever he wants.

Why does that matter to us? If you have a mission to carry out, it's good to know your boss has the authority to back you up.

Jesus earned that authority. Before he came into the world 2,000 years ago, all the nations stood under God's wrath, cursed for their rebellion against him. Satan stood as the accuser, pointing out that humanity was guilty of sin and deserved hell. Where sin is involved, someone has to pay.

Sin can only be covered over with the blood of death. Throughout the many years that span the Old Testament, it was the sacrificial blood of animals that served as the temporary payment for sin. When Christ came, *he* became the permanent sacrificial lamb who takes away the sins of the world. He died in our place and paid our sin debt. We no longer had to repeatedly offer blood sacrifices to atone for our sin. Christ's death covered us for all time and silenced all Satan's accusations against us. That's not just good news. That's *really* good news. Sin, death, and Satan have been conquered. Our debt is paid. A new day has dawned!

We pursue our mission because Jesus commissioned us to *share* this good news, just as he commissioned his original disciples to do.

Jesus made clear every disciple of his was to, *"Go therefore and make disciples of all nations."* (Matthew 28:19) It's not a suggestion. It's a mandate given to you personally, to me personally. He entrusted to us the life-changing message that can save people's lives for all eternity. If we understand what's at stake and what it means to him, then we'll realize why he expects us to *accept* the assignment with a grateful heart, thankful for the privilege of partnering with him.

We pursue our mission because we've been promised everything we need to carry out our mission. We have no excuse.

Once we place our trust in Christ, we have the authority, the mandate, and the backup to make disciples as we go about the daily act of living our lives. Jesus basically says, "You can do this! I've got you covered."

The "What" of Our Mission

What, then, does it look like to live out this high calling? Our Mission Statement uses three action verbs that give us direction.

Develop

In Matthew 28:19 Jesus said, *"Make disciples of all nations,* **baptizing** *them...***teaching** *them to observe all that I have commanded you."*

Baptize. Teach. Those are our key words related to developing disciples. When a person hears the good news of the gospel and by God's grace makes the decision to turn from sin and choose Christ as his or her Savior, baptism is a sign and seal of the inward cleansing the person has received by faith and their initiation into the visible church. Likewise, the *children* of believers are baptized as a sign of God's covenant promises, held out to all who believe. And they, likewise, receive all the benefits of Christ through faith in him. In other words, baptism is about being identified with Christ and his people, the church, and is a significant part of developing disciples.

The next step in building disciples is teaching. Christianity is not one *part* of your life. It's a *way* of life, the way of Jesus. It's how we live. When we are reborn into God's family, there's learning to be done, to understand our new life.

Covenant is intentionally a teaching church. Through Sunday sermons and Bible classes through the week and Bible studies and small groups at church and in homes, we learn the way of Jesus.

Teaching is something that followers of Jesus welcome. Our grateful hearts want to know what God has done for us and what God expects of us, so we can fully live out the life he planned for us.

Deploy

When Jesus instructed us to make disciples of all nations, he wasn't just talking about sending missionaries to some far-flung country like Kenya or India. He meant to mobilize *every* believer, *every* day, *everywhere* they go—in our families, our community, and our world—to serve the body of Christ and share the good news. Today. Tomorrow. Every day until Jesus returns. Here. There. Everywhere.

Disciple

There's a cyclical nature and rhythm to the life of a disciple. We've synthesized it into the three verbs of our Mission Statement—Develop, Deploy, Disciple. We **develop** initially, through our salvation experience and baptism, followed by the ongoing growth that occurs through teaching. We are then **deployed** (released) into the world, where Jesus expects us to replicate what happened to us—to **disciple** others through the proclamation of the gospel, so more disciples will be baptized and learn the way of Christ. It's what we do. Like ever-widening ripples when you throw a stone into water, the good news spreads.

It starts with our own families: Husbands and wives making disciples of one another, moms and dads making disciples of their children. The circle widens to our community: tennis friends, a mom's group, golfing buddies, coworkers, and neighbors. And finally, it extends to the world, through our participation in cross-cultural missions worldwide.

**If you are a disciple,
you are called to be a disciple-maker.**

Are you thinking, "I'm not developed enough *myself* to be able to deploy and make other disciples of Jesus?"

Not true.

**You don't need to be fully *developed*
in order to make disciples.
You only need to be fully *devoted*.**

You have good news to share. Jesus trusts you to do the job and promises to have your back. If your next thought is, "Then show me how to do it," that's the purpose of this book. Not only does our Mission Statement have a certain rhythm to it, so does discipleship. Read on.

The "How" of Our Mission

Christian communities throughout history often organized around a prescribed way of living that accelerated their ability to accomplish their mission. The Benedictines had their Rule of Life, a set of precepts that covered their life in community. In most religious communities these principles for living out faith are unstated. They're "caught" more often than taught.

However, we want everyone who is part of the family of faith to feel at home right away at Covenant. Some people reading this book grew up in church settings, but others had no faith tradition or concept of what it meant to be a follower of Christ. To you, the new life of faith may seem mysterious and a bit overwhelming.

We don't want you to guess what we're about. That's why we developed our rhythm or "rule" for living out our faith together in community. It's built around four key disciplines:

Worship * Grow * Serve * Go

A "rhythm" speaks to regularity, something you can count on, set your watch or calendar by. We believe these four disciplines represent a kind of shorthand for our life together. Taken together, they will help us fulfill our mission to **develop, deploy, and disciple.**

In the following chapters, we look at these four components in greater detail. Here's a preview:

Worship

God made us for worship. We gather on Sunday mornings to worship corporately with the Covenant family. We worship regularly with our family at home. We worship daily in our times alone with the Lord. In fact, worship finds expression in every part of our life. **Disciples worship.** We'll dig deeper into this in the next couple chapters.

Grow

Growth doesn't happen by accident. Did you ever meet an athlete who ran a marathon without the proper training, diet, and exercise?

Part of our weekly rhythm at Covenant involves intentional Bible study with at least one other believer in many possible settings. **Disciples grow.** The Holy Spirit wants to help. We'll discuss this in more detail in Chapters Four and Five.

Serve

God has gifted every disciple of Jesus. You may not yet know what your gifts are, but you have them. We all get some. We just don't all get the same ones. If you don't know yours, we'll help you uncover them.

God expects you to wisely steward the time, talents and treasure you've been given. Part of our rhythm at Covenant is for every believer to find a way to use his or her time, talents, and treasure to serve Christ and our community every week in some capacity. **Disciples serve.** Chapters Six and Seven will address this.

Go

Disciples are people on the move. As we've already mentioned, they *go* take the gospel to their family, community, and world. They *go* make disciples. They *go* and do good works in Jesus's name. There are no couch potatoes in God's family. **Disciples go**. We address this in Chapters Eight and Nine.

*　　*　　*

Think about a car with four wheels. If any one is missing, it's hard to go anywhere. Even more so if two or more wheels are missing.

- If all we're doing is worshiping on Sundays but we're not serving others or taking the gospel to the world, we're not living the mission.
- If we're serving at the church six days a week but not allowing God's Word to dwell in us richly, we're not living the mission.

- If we've never had our neighbors over for dinner or if we have no relationships with those who don't share our faith, we're not living out the mission.
- If all we do is mingle with non-Christians and rarely take part of corporate worship, we're not living the mission.

It all matters.

It's a high bar. But, doing it together empowered by the gospel, it can happen. God will be honored. We will be living the life God intended. The world around us will change. *We* will change.

Make no mistake. This is not about us jumping through some clever hoops so God will love us or answer all our prayers. We choose to live this rhythm out of grateful hearts that have been gripped by the unconditional love of an unchanging God, who stopped at nothing to bring us to himself. That's good news. That's the gospel.

**It's the astounding news
that the only One who deserved heaven
endured the wrath of hell instead,
so we who deserved the wrath of hell
would be assured we will only experience heaven.**

All the bad news of this world—death, ruin, decay, and darkness—is being *undone* through the work of Christ and his followers who choose to be gospel-centered instead of self-centered.

The only way we can fail in this mission is not to participate. Jesus has promised that, as we go out in his name, he will work in us by his Spirit—taking away our fears, making us bold, giving us love for the lost and an unconquerable confidence in the power of the gospel to bring people from death to life! Are you "all in"? Then read on.

BETWEEN YOU AND GOD

1. As you scan back through this chapter, write down what most excites you about this way of looking at discipleship and what may feel overwhelming or unrealistic at this season in your life. Then, after you've finished reading the book, review your comments here and see what's changed or whether you still feel the same way. God wants to change all of us. Tell him how you would like to be changed and ask for his help. Expect him to do something special.

2. Do you have particular spiritual practices that are your "rhythm" for spiritual growth? Write down what works and what parts have always felt harder. Talk it over with God.

3. Was there a particular point made in this chapter that resonated with you as something you feel convicted to act on? Write it down, along with a first step you could take to act on what you've read.

Chapter 2

WORSHIP

In the Sanctuary, In the Living Room, In the Closet

"Most middle-class Americans tend to worship their work,
to work at their play, and to play at their worship."[1]
Gordon Dahl

These words were written more than 50 years ago and they're even truer today. What happens when we *worship* our work and *play* at our worship? Eventually, we feel the pain of an empty soul. Then, to ease the pain, we fill our lives with noise and distractions.

Many years ago, Blaise Pascal observed, "Take away their diversion and you will find them bored to extremity. Then they sense their emptiness without recognizing it rationally. For nothing can be more miserable than to be intolerably depressed as soon as one is reduced to introspection with no means of distraction."[2]

In other words, to avoid feeling the emptiness of our souls, we distract ourselves with more work and more play, when what we need is worship, appropriately directed.

Worship boils down to this:

- Who or what do we love?
- Who or in what do we trust?
- Who do we obey?
- What gives us a sense of significance and meaning?

As the acclaimed novelist, Fyodor Dostoyevsky wrote, "So long as man remains free, he strives for nothing so incessantly and so painfully as to find someone to worship."[3]

Our sinful nature is naturally inclined to worship something that doesn't require us to repent of our sin and rebellion, so we make gods of things like our work, family, money, and pleasure. They aren't innately bad. They just aren't capable of doing the heavy lifting when it comes to fulfilling our deepest longings for love, trust, security, and peace of mind. Delivering soul satisfaction is out of their league.

Eventually, they fail us or we fail them and we move on.

The problem is not worship.
Worship *is* the answer for hungry souls.
But it requires the right *object* of worship.

The Bible teaches that the deepest needs of our heart can only be met in God. Only he is worthy of our worship and only he can deliver true soul satisfaction.

That's why our Rhythm of Discipleship begins with worship—biblical worship *in the sanctuary, in the living room, and in the closet*—a concept we'll describe later in more detail.

To worship means we start with a few important premises:

- There is an all-powerful, all-knowing, all-loving, personal God, carrying out his holy will every moment of every day.
- He is revealed to us in the Bible and worthy of worship.
- I am not him.
- Neither are you.

Psalm 63 is a great place to explore what happens next. It talks about the *fuel* of worship, the *object* of worship, and the *action* of worship.

The FUEL of Worship

King David wrote Psalm 63 in the wilderness of Judah, an empty barren place that, coincidentally, also reflected the condition of his soul at that moment. David wrote, *"My soul thirsts for you; my flesh faints for you, as in a dry and weary land where there is no water."* (Psalm 63:1)

He should have been in Jerusalem ruling over his people. Instead, his son Absalom had pulled off a palace coup and David was hiding out in the desert, contemplating his next move. All the activities and responsibilities were gone that normally would have filled his day. He was alone and bereft.

What do people do when they find themselves in this condition? Again, Pascal's words summarize David's condition in this moment:

> Man finds nothing so intolerable as to be in a state of absolute rest, without exercising any passions, being unemployed, having no diversion, and living without any effort. It is then that he thinks he faces emptiness, loneliness, a sense of inadequacy, feeling dependent, helpless, and living a meaningless life. Then there wells up from the depths of his being a sense of boredom, pessimism, depression, frustration, resentment, and despair.[4]

Earlier in David's life, after sending his soldiers off to war, he faced a similar moment. He wandered onto his rooftop, perhaps bored, and saw beautiful Bathsheba bathing nearby. In that moment he believed that indulging the lust of his body would quench the thirst of his soul.

But by the time David wrote Psalm 63 in the wilderness, he finally recognized his thirst for what it was: a thirst for the infinite that nothing finite could satisfy. *"O God, you are my God; earnestly I seek you."* (Psalm 63:1)

This is the essence of biblical worship:
a thirsty soul seeking the God who gives living water.

Thirst isn't wrong. It's real. What's wrong is that we don't recognize it for what it is and then we run to fountains that can't satisfy. The same thirst that drives you to overeat, to hoard, to seek affirmation in all the wrong places, to pursue pornography, to cut yourself, to overachieve, is the same thirst that can lead you to Jesus.

The next time you're hungry or thirsty for what can't satisfy, stop! Name what you're feeling, remind yourself that only God can quench your *soul* thirst.

Thirst can *fuel* worship. Come thirsty!
Drink deeply of God's *living* water.

The OBJECT of Worship

Once David recognized his thirst, he began to think back on all the times he had worshiped with God's people and been reminded who God was: *"So I have looked upon you in the sanctuary, beholding your power and glory."* (Psalm 63:2)

- He remembered how God's power created the heavens and the earth and everything in them.
- He remembered how God's power defeated the Egyptians and delivered Israel from captivity, then parted the Red Sea, so the people could walk on dry land.

- He remembered how God's power gave him victory over Goliath and later made a king out of a shepherd boy.
- He remembered how the power of God gave him comfort in the midst of his helplessness and weakness.

The *object of* David's worship was Almighty God—substantial, weighty, solid, and glorious to behold! To worship such a beautiful and powerful God filled his soul with relief. In Psalm 63:3 David writes, *"Because your steadfast love is better than life, my lips will praise you."*

Today, people often move from church to church not satisfied with the worship (by which they generally mean not satisfied with the *music*). Good music *can* play an important role in facilitating worship and we highly value the artistic excellence of our worship teams at Covenant. However, anyone who has ever worshiped in a Third World country with off-key singers and out-of-tune instruments knows that good worship can happen without good music. The style, the aesthetics, and the excellence of the music are not to be the *object* of our worship, nor are they an essential criterion for good worship. It is God himself who deserves our full attention.

Are you a worshiper of worship or a worshiper of God? Worship the God of glory, whose great love for us played out on the cross for all to see. Make *him* the object of your worship.

The ACTION of Worship

When your thirsty soul finds satisfaction in God, action follows. In Psalm 63:3-4, David *beholds* God and his holy attributes and *responds* with prayer and praise, using body language and words to communicate his sentiments. *"My lips will praise you. So I will bless you as long as I live; in your name, I will lift up my hands."*

In verses 5-6 he continues, *"My mouth will praise you with joyful lips when I remember you upon my bed and meditate on you in the watches of the night."*

Meditation is not a practice reserved for super spiritual people. It's simply another way to behold God. To meditate is to think about who God is and what he's like. As we turn the truth about him over and over in our minds, it takes root in our heart and prayer and praise naturally follow.

In our worship services, we constantly behold and respond. When we read Scripture, when I preach, when we present truth in song, you're invited to *behold* your God. When you sing, when you raise your hands, when you pray, when you walk in obedience, you *respond*.

The Psalms are filled with different ways we can respond in worship: praise, bless, lift up hands, sing for joy, clap, shout, fall on your face, dance, bring an offering, and more. We ought to find ourselves from time to time longing for a greater ability to express our love and gratitude more suitably to him.

> *No praise is high enough, no thanks is deep enough,*
> *no life is long enough, to tell of all You've done.*
> *No shout is loud enough, no words are strong enough,*
> *no song is sweet enough, to sing Your love.*[5]

Then, when our thirst is quenched and our hearts are full, it's human nature to want to share what delights us. I love to hike in the mountains and take in the beautiful scenery, but I love it even more when my wife Emily and I can see it together. I love to see a great movie, but I love it even more when I can to share it with people I love.

In the same way, I love to delight in the greatness and glory of God, but I love it even more when others behold him and respond as well. That's why I'm sharing these principles with you, so we can enthusiastically worship our great God together.

The PLACE Where We Worship

Historically, believers have worshiped in three arenas of life:

- Together with other believers in the sanctuary
- With our families in our homes
- By ourselves, alone with God

The Westminster Confession of Faith, one of the primary documents used by Presbyterians to summarize what the Bible teaches, promoted this idea more than 500 years ago, capturing what the Church has believed across the ages:

> God is to be worshiped everywhere, in spirit and truth; as in *private families* daily, and in secret, *each one by himself*; so, more solemnly in the *public assemblies*, which are not carelessly or willfully to be neglected, or forsaken.
> Westminster Confession of Faith 21.6

Worship...In the Sanctuary

From the earliest days of history, God's people have gathered at appointed times for praise, prayer, the ministry of the Word, and the administration of the sacraments. These are the primary means of grace and growth in the Christian life. Thus, the cornerstone of discipleship has always been the weekly gathering of the church for corporate worship.

From the time of the New Testament, Christians have celebrated corporate worship on this first day of the week, often called The Lord's Day.

- It's on this day that Jesus rose from the dead.
- It's when Jesus met his two disciples on the road to Emmaus, explained the Scriptures, and broke bread with them.

- It was the day Jesus poured out his Holy Spirit—the Day of Pentecost.
- It was on this day Christians gathered to celebrate the Lord's Supper and take up a collection for the saints in Jerusalem.

The weekly worship of the church on Sunday is the pinnacle of our worship on earth. Gathered in Jesus's name, beholding and responding to God in worship, we are closer to heaven than at any other time.

Why is it so important to worship corporately? Here we find the presence and love of others that we don't have when we're alone. We're able to build up each other using our spiritual gifts, which we can't do when we're alone.

There's an unfortunate phenomenon taking place in the modern church today that most of church history knows nothing about. It's the elevation of *private* worship over the *public* worship of God.

The idea that I should worship God on my own and, therefore, not need to be part of a local church is completely foreign to the Scriptures. Each one of us needs to be under the authority and shepherding care of elders and to sit under the sound preaching of the Word.

The most important thing you can do to feed your soul is to be present in corporate worship every Sunday. Nevertheless, our worship is not limited to Sundays. Worship *in the sanctuary* generally flows out of worship *in the living room,* and *in the closet.*

Worship...In the Living Room

Here we're talking about worship at home with your family or Christian housemates, if you have them.

When I think of worship in the family, I'm reminded of a poster a friend gave me that says, *"As for me and my house, we will serve the Lord and cheer for the West Virginia Mountaineers."* Sometimes I fear I lead my family to *worship* the Mountaineers and only *cheer* for the Lord!

These days the number of families who worship together on a regular basis in the home is pretty small, but that was not always the case. In fact, we moderns are an anomaly.

As one writer reports, "So seriously did the Puritans take the duty of family worship that they regarded the neglect of family devotion and catechism to be 'covenant-breaking with God, and betraying the souls of their children to the devil.'"[6]

Sound severe? It's a reminder to us that we have a holy obligation as parents to raise our children in the nurture and admonition of the Lord.

What does family worship look like? It's not terribly complicated. In our family, we usually take time in the morning to read some passage of Scripture or talk about some scriptural truth, perhaps sing a song or psalm and then pray. In the evening we'll typically read from a children's Bible, sing a song of praise and pray. It calls us back together, reminding us of who we are, why we're here, and where soul-satisfaction is found. We may miss a morning, an evening, or an entire day, but we keep coming back to it.

Our families should be our first small group and discipleship priority. But, as mentioned earlier, family worship does not trump corporate worship on Sunday.

In *Give Praise to God: A Vision for Reforming Worship,* the authors remind us, "The first and primary key to your family's spiritual health is a commitment to the weekly public worship services of the church. The most important single commitment you must make to ensure your family's spiritual well-being is to regular, consistent attendance at public worship."[7]

Worship…In the Closet

Here we're talking about a daily time alone with God. There's no magic length of time or place prescribed in Scripture for it. Everyone must identify what works for them. It simply means taking regular time apart, undistracted, when you can read and meditate on scripture, pour out your heart's concerns in prayer, confess your sins, and express your personal gratitude for what the Lord has done for you and in you.

It's in this private alone time with the Lord that we have opportunity to linger in our beholding of God and to worship in the most personal of ways. While corporate worship is still most important, our experience in corporate and family worship is greatly influenced by what has happened during our *worship in the closet.*

*   *   *

Can you see why at Covenant we believe *worship* is crucial to our rhythm of discipleship? Jesus calls us to come and find what we're looking for in him: *"Let the one who is thirsty come; let the one who desires take the water of life without price."* (Revelation 22:17)

Come thirsty! Let God quench your thirst with his living water. Behold. Respond. Everywhere! In the sanctuary, in the living room, and in the closet.

BETWEEN YOU AND GOD

1. If worship boils down to what you love and what gives your life meaning and significance, what do *you* love? Has your family or your career or your lifestyle taken on more importance than God? What needs to change? What steps will you take to change?

2. Do you think of worship as an everyday, everywhere spiritual discipline? Name a place in your life where you'd like to incorporate some spontaneous worship—perhaps driving in your car or walking the dog.

3. How do you think a different attitude toward worship could change your relationship to God and to other people?

---

[1] Gordon Dahl, *Work, Play and Worship in a Leisure-Oriented Society* (Augsburg Publishing House, 1972).

[2] Blaise Pascal, *Pensees and the Provincial Letters* (Random House, 1941), #164.

[3] Fyodor Dostoyevsky, *The Brothers Karamazov* (The New American Library, 1962), 234.

[4] Pascal, #131.

[5] "Sooner Count the Stars" by Doug Plank, Steve and Vikki Cook, *Sovereign Grace Worship*.

[6] Joel R. Beeke and Mark Jones, *A Puritan Theology* (Reformation Heritage Books, 2012), 864.

[7] J. Ligon Duncan III and Terry L. Johnson, "A Call to Family Worship" in *Give Praise to God: A Vision for Reforming Worship* (P & R Publishing, 2003), 329.

Chapter 3

WORSHIP

In All of Life

In his famous commencement speech at Kenyon College, the late author David Foster Wallace told the following parable: "There are these two young fish swimming along and they happen to meet an older fish, swimming the other way, who nods at them and says, 'Morning, boys. How's the water?' And the two young fish swim on for a bit, and then eventually one of them looks over at the other and goes, 'What the hell is water?'"[1]

The parable highlights an important life lesson:

**The things that influence us the most
are usually the things of which we're least aware.**

You and I live immersed in our own version of "water." The way we think, the way we act, and the things we desire, are not developed in a vacuum but rather in the families and cultural settings we inhabit day in and day out. We are immersed in a world of water that shapes how we see and experience the world. It shapes our desires and creates for us a vision of what represents "the good life."

Philosopher and theologian James K.A. Smith writes, "It is a picture of flourishing that we imagine in a visceral, often-unarticulated way—a vague yet attractive sense of where we think true happiness is found."[2]

Whether you've ever said it out loud or not, you probably have a picture in your mind of what the good life looks like for *you*. And every day by your actions you're spending your life betting on the hope that it's true.

Do you realize that what you're living for isn't necessarily what your brain *thinks* it's living for? It's really what you *long for* in the depths of your heart. In fact, your *subconscious* decisions, even more than your *conscious* decisions, are what move you toward that vision of true happiness.

What you *long* for is what you worship.

So are you worshiping the right things? Are you worshiping what you *think* you're worshiping? The decisions and actions you make day-to-day, such as the way you spend your time and money, help you identify what you truly worship. That means your idealized picture of human flourishing had better be accurate. If it isn't, then when you achieve it, you will be devastated.

Again, David Foster Wallace, who was not a Christian, said:

> In the day-to-day trenches of adult life, there is no such thing as atheism.
>
> There is no such thing as not worshiping. Everybody worships. The only choice we get is what to worship. And an outstanding reason for choosing some sort of god or spiritual-type thing to worship...is that pretty much anything else you worship will eat you alive.

If you worship money and things...then you will never have enough. Never feel you have enough. It's the truth. Worship your own body and beauty and sexual allure and you will always feel ugly, and when time and age start showing, you will die a million deaths before they finally plant you. ... Worship power and you will feel weak and afraid, and you will need ever more power over others to keep the fear at bay. Worship your intellect, being seen as smart, and you will end up feeling stupid, a fraud, always on the verge of being found out.[3]

Essentially he's saying it's better to worship a spiritual god than something like money or beauty because you'll never get what you're looking for from them.

Here's where Wallace is most insightful: "The insidious thing about these forms of worship is not that they're evil or sinful; it is that they are unconscious. They are default settings. They're the kind of worship you just gradually slip into, day after day, getting more and more selective about what you see and how you measure value without ever being fully aware that that's what you're doing."[4]

As Wallace so helpfully points out, you're *already* living a life of worship. If you're not intentional about *what* you're worshiping day-to-day, you will gradually slip into worshiping what the culture around you is worshiping, without even knowing it. If you worship power, money, beauty and so on, ultimately you will find yourself unsatisfied.

Do you know what you worship? Look at your life. Your life is a reflection of what you love the most. At Covenant, we talk about living a life of *biblical* worship that's part of an intentional rhythm of discipleship. We believe true human flourishing comes when we worship the God revealed in the Bible. So let's talk about God's alternative for worship.

In the last chapter, we talked about *where* we should worship God (in the sanctuary, in the living room, and in the closet). Now let's talk about what *characteristics* mark a life of biblical worship.

A life of biblical worship is a sacrificial, logical, radical, transformational response to God's mercies.

The apostle Paul—a smart, articulate explainer of the life of faith—writes passionately about this kind of worship in Romans 12.

Biblical Worship is SACRIFICIAL

Chapter 12 represents a turning point in the book of Romans. Up to this point, the apostle Paul has been laying out the doctrinal foundation for the rest of the book, which in Chapter 12 gets totally practical. It's as if Paul is saying, "Here's how all this amazing theological truth should find expression in your day-to-day lives."

"I appeal to you, therefore, brothers, by the mercies of God, to present your bodies as a living sacrifice, holy and acceptable to God, which is your spiritual worship." (Romans 12:1) Paul pleads with these Christians, in light of everything that's been said up to now about justification by faith, grace, election, and salvation, to *do* something in response.

"Present your bodies"

A life of biblical worship, Paul says, means you present your entire body to God for his use. This language probably shocked Paul's Greco-Roman audience who had been raised to believe that the body and physicality were bad and that spirituality was something primarily to do with the mind and soul.

Sometimes we preachers accentuate this by talking about how you should give your *heart* to God. That sentiment is true enough, but according to Paul, we ought just as frequently to say that you need to give your *body* to God. The late British theologian John Stott writes, "No worship is pleasing to God which is purely inward, abstract and mystical; it must express itself in concrete acts of service performed by our bodies."

Paul expresses a similar sentiment in Romans 6:12-13: *"Do not present your members [parts of your body] to sin as instruments for unrighteousness, but present yourselves to God as those who have been brought from death to life, and your members to God as instruments for righteousness."*

Our bodies, formerly used in the worship of false gods and in the service of sin, are now to be presented to God for *his* use, to serve what is good and right.

"As a living sacrifice"

Our bodies are to be presented as a living sacrifice. Paul here is using Old Testament worship language. In the Old Testament, an animal sacrifice offered to God was killed. However, with Christ's death on the cross, a blood sacrifice was no longer necessary, because Christ paid our sin once for all.

Therefore, Paul says you don't have to lay down your life for Christ *in death*. Instead, lay down your life for Christ *in life*. God doesn't want your money or your time without *you*. *You* are the one for whom Jesus died. *You* are the one he loves. Your stuff is no substitute for you.

What does it mean, then, to present yourself as a living sacrifice? It means to be fully surrendered to God for his purposes. At Covenant, we say it means to be a fully devoted follower of Christ. Your whole life and everything in your life is offered to him for his use.

For those who have trusted in Christ for their salvation, the Bible says we are already holy and acceptable to him, because of Christ. But a life of biblical worship means we daily make ourselves *available* to God, no matter the demand, no matter the cost. Rick Warren, the author of *The Purpose-Driven Life,* says, "We've all surrendered to something. Why not God?"

Marcie Erickson, our own missionary to Ethiopia, shared an illustration of this that touched me deeply. She says she's seen believers with so little money but so full of love for God that they literally put themselves in the offering baskets. That's the picture! Giving God not just my tithe, but also my whole self, not just my presence in church on Sunday, but also every moment of my life. It's saying, "I'm all yours, God, and I'm all in." It's *sacrificial* worship.

Biblical Worship is LOGICAL

Go back and look at the opening line of Romans 12 that I passed over earlier. There we see the motive for a life of worshiping the God of the Bible. We read, *"I appeal to you, therefore, brothers, by the mercies of God."*

"By the mercies of God"

What are the mercies of God upon which Paul is basing his appeal to us? Paul speaks passionately about God's mercies in Romans 1-11. In short, when Christ became the object of God's wrath and paid our sin debt on the cross, *we* became the objects of God's mercy.

Don't confuse the order here. Paul doesn't say, present yourself to God and *then* you will receive his mercy—as if our actions prompt God's mercy, like a transaction where I give something to get something. Rather, he says, having *received* God's mercies (with no strings attached), *now* present yourself to God.

"Which is your spiritual worship"

This phrase is notoriously difficult to translate into English. The simple form of the Greek word translated here as "spiritual," is often translated as "rational or reasonable." In other words, without God's prior display of mercy, it might seem irrational to give our all to him. But when we grasp the full extent of God's mercies, then, Paul says, giving our whole lives to God is a completely logical and reasonable response.

Beloved Presbyterian pastor and author Tim Keller is helpful here as he often is: "Once you have a good view of God's mercy, anything less than a total, complete sacrifice of yourself to God is completely irrational. If you give yourself partially or half-heartedly, you are simply not thinking; you are not looking at what Jesus did. If what he did does not move you or break the ice over your soul, you must ask yourself if you have ever understood the gospel."[5]

Do you know the gospel? It is the message that has captivated the hearts of believers for more than 2,000 years? The message that says though Christ was rich he became poor in every way so that we who were poor could be made rich in every way? The message that says he who had no sin became sin for us, so that we could become the righteousness of God? When we fully grasp the love and mercy shown to us by Christ's actions on our behalf, we'll say, "Why would I not put my whole life in his hands?" To refuse is irrational! It means I trust someone or something other than the God who has loved me with an everlasting love.

A life of biblical worship is *logical.*

Biblical Worship is RADICAL

In Romans 12:2, Paul begins to break down for us how this life of biblical worship works itself out in daily life. He says, "Do not be conformed to this world." Literally, do not be conformed to this age.

In the words of New Testament scholar Doug Moo, this age, "...is the sin-dominated, death-producing realm in which all people included in Adam's fall naturally belong."[6] It is the world that stands opposed to God.

The world we live in wants to press us into its mold, to make us think like it thinks and to live life without regard to the God who reigns over it all. As described earlier, this is the "water" (the environment) we live in every day and mostly don't notice.

But there's good news! Galatians 1:4 teaches us that Christ "gave himself for our sins to deliver us from the present evil age." However, there's a problem:

Although we have been delivered from the *dominion* of this present evil age, we are not free of its *influence*.

We still must be alert to the subtle ways it presses us to conform.

In *Give Praise to God,* an anthology of writings about worship, Christian apologist William Edgar tells the story of Petrov, a prisoner in a work camp that was part of the Gulag prison labor camps under the old Soviets. Each day, he went to work in a designated area and then returned through a checkpoint to his barracks.

One evening he returned to his barracks with a wheelbarrow containing a large sack. At the checkpoint, the guard stopped him and asked what he was stealing from the work site in that sack. Petrov protested that he was not stealing a thing and that the bag contained only sawdust. The guard opened it up, and sure enough, it contained only sawdust.

The next evening, the same thing happened. The guard stopped the inmate with his wheelbarrow and sack, but, again, all he could find was sawdust. This routine repeated itself several evenings in a row until finally, the exasperated guard told Petrov he knew he was stealing something, but couldn't decide what it was. He promised not to denounce Petrov if only he would confess.

"Wheelbarrows, sir, I am stealing wheelbarrows," the clever prisoner admitted.

Edgar, reflecting on this parable, writes that something similar can happen to us in our Christian lives. "We think we are resisting the world because we refuse to be taken in by the content of the world's ways. Yet we are nevertheless seduced by the form, the container which shapes that content."[7]

For example, we may strenuously avoid misusing church funds but overlook the fact that we're running the church like a corporation, where the spreadsheet rules and does not "factor in" God. Or, we who are parents may read our children Bible stories about how God promises to meet our financial needs, and then we frantically pursue more income and status as if that's what matters most and it's all up to us to meet our needs. We may have Bible verses on every wall in our home about loving others and putting God first, yet we live a daily rhythm that reinforces self-centeredness rather than sacrifice.[8]

James K.A. Smith writes, "Each household and family does well to take an audit of its daily routines. ... What story is carried in those rhythms? What vision of the good life is carried in those practices?"[9] We may not realize we inadvertently impress the world's values on our families through the forms and rhythms we embrace, even if we're avoiding the content itself. Bottom line? When we live as people who've been set free from the spirit of our age, our lives may, in fact, appear somewhat radical. But living a life of biblical worship means we must resist conforming to the "water" of this age.

A word of caution is appropriate here for you mass consumers of news media. It is true that some left-leaning news media try to conform you to their way of thinking, so you decide not to watch or listen to them (or, when you do, it's with a very critical eye). But the right-leaning conservative news media are doing the exact same thing. The conservative news media present a vision of human flourishing that's not the same one presented in the Bible.

Both the conservative and liberal news media present a vision that has *some* things in common with the Bible. But we're not to be conformed to *either* one of them because they're both of "this age." God calls us to be conformed to the age to come.

I encourage you to read books by people who don't live in our current time and culture. For example, reading the words of people like 12th-century Catholic monk Bernard of Clairvaux or 21st-century Chinese house church leader Brother Yun offers a more objective voice from outside our own culture and can help us recognize more clearly the "water" we're living in.

Of course, the Bible itself shines the best spotlight on this age and is always our best resource for navigating the world in which we live. In the end, if we consciously work hard not to conform to this age, our lives *will* appear radical. It's part of what it means to be transformed by God into people who truly represent him.

Biblical Worship is TRANSFORMATIONAL

The apostle Paul takes biblical worship a step further in Romans 12:2, writing, *"Do not be conformed to this world, but be transformed by the renewal of your mind, that by testing you may discern what is the will of God, what is good and acceptable and perfect."*

Paul nets it out. Either our convictions and values and vision for flourishing come from the world or they come from our minds that have been renewed by God's truth. There is no third option.

Make no mistake, though. Although we've been saved by God and rescued from all that stands opposed to God, **our transformation takes time**. Our hearts, minds, and bodies must develop the habit of turning heavenward for guidance. The transforming power of the gospel must find its way into every nook and cranny of our lives.

As we learn more what God loves and hates, we increasingly learn to think like him and make the kind of choices he would make. It becomes easier to discern God's will and know what is "good and acceptable and perfect" in any situation.

As we live all of life this way, "the age to come" (God's kingdom and ways) increasingly transforms the "water" of this age we're living in. That's when our lives become a true offering to God.

One of my favorite heroes from history is Eric Liddell. Those familiar with the movie "Chariots of Fire" will remember Liddell as the man who refused to run on Sunday, even when it meant not running the 100-meter sprint, an event in which he was a sure bet to win Olympic gold. Eric was a man who did not conform to the age in which he lived. He lived with a renewed, transformed mind and was always bringing transformation to the world around him.

He frequently talked about this idea of offering ourselves wholly to God by using the language of surrender. He said, "Surrender means that we are prepared to follow God's guidance, wherever or however He guides, no matter what the cost." Radical, whole-hearted devotion was the mark of Eric's life.

We may or may not agree with his conviction about not running on Sundays, but we can all appreciate his refusal to conform to the world's expectations, even under immense social and political pressure.

In those same 1924 Olympic games in which he withdrew from the 100-meter race because it was being held on Sunday, Liddell entered the 400-meter race—a race that no one believed he could win. He shocked the world and brought glory to his God when he not only won the gold medal but also set a world record in the process.

Then, while at the height of his running career, Eric shocked the world a second time by leaving his home in Scotland to serve as a missionary to China. Nevertheless, as had been the pattern of his entire life, he continued to bring heavenly transformation, no matter the circumstances in which he found himself.

Eventually, he was sent to a Japanese internment camp where on February 21, 1945, he died for Christ. With his last words, he again repeated the secret to his life of worship. "It is complete surrender."

Only a heart gripped by the mercy and grace of God can understand the joy of that kind of radical devotion. Consider the mercies of our God and, like the apostle Paul, like Eric Liddell and, like so many others, give your whole self to him. It's a logical, radical, transformational thing to do. It's biblical worship *with all your life.*

BETWEEN YOU AND GOD

1. Write down four or five things that represent "the good life" for you—things you are willing to work hard for and invest yourself in. Have you made a god of any of these things?

2. Using this chapter as a guide, name in what ways, if any, your worship is sacrificial, logical, radical, or transformational. In which of these areas would you like to grow? Write down one thing you might do to achieve that goal.

3. Do you remember how you felt when you first made the decision to follow Christ? Do a heart check. Is your current passion for worship and spiritual growth still burning strong? Talk over with God about what has changed and ask his help in those areas where you may feel your zeal has "cooled."

----

[1]David Foster Wallace, "Plain Old Untrendy Troubles and Emotions," *The Guardian*, September 20, 2008.

[2]James K.A. Smith, *You Are What You Love: The Spiritual Power of Habit,* (Baker, 2016), 11.

[3]Wallace, Commencement Speech, Kenyon College, 2005, https://www.youtube.com/watch?v=IYGaXzJGVAQ

[4]Wallace, Kenyon College speech, 2005.

[5]Tim Keller, *Romans 8-16 For You* (The Good Book Company, 2014), 106.

[6]Douglas Moo, *The Epistle to the Romans* (Wm. B. Eerdmans Publishing Co., 1996), 755.

[7]William Edgar, "Worship in All of Life," *Give Praise to God: A Vision for Reforming Worship* (P & R Publishing, 2003), 346-47.

[8]Smith, 127.

[9]Smith, 128.

Chapter 4

GROW

In Community, Through the Word, By the Spirit

Grandfathers are known for saying wise things. My Papaw Bob used to say, tongue-in-cheek, "Nobody's perfect except for me and you...and I'm not so sure about you." We all tend to think that way about one another, don't we?

It's easy to see that the people *around* us need to grow. You may be *sure* your spouse needs to grow and they surely do. And, parents, I know you want your children to grow in faith. That's why you bring them to Sunday School. But do you realize that perhaps the single biggest factor influencing your spouse or your children's spiritual growth is your *own* growth as a Christian? If you are honest enough to admit you need to grow, the question is: what are you doing about it?

At Covenant, we think spiritual growth is so important it's one of the four components of our Worship, Grow, Serve, and Go Rhythm of Discipleship. So let's break down how growth happens in the Christian life. This isn't everything that needs to be said about growth, but it will give you a strong foundation. It starts with this core principle:

Christians grow *in* community,
***through* the Word,**
***by* the Spirit.**

Let's start with community. Do you have a realistic picture of Christian community? Typically, we imagine a group of people happily sitting around a living room, looking at their Bibles together, and going deep with the Lord in a kind of Kumbaya moment. It happens. But sometimes it doesn't.

Emily and I were in ministry in Dallas before we came to Naples. One evening we were invited over to the home of a wonderful older couple that, incidentally, had no children. They had invited us and other friends to their house for a Christmas party. We took Hudson with us (our only child at the time). He was just over a year old.

It was a lovely home, great guests. We were all sitting around the living room having that wonderful Kumbaya moment I mentioned, sharing stories. Our hostess was telling us about a snow globe that was on the coffee table. It was a gift from an internationally acclaimed country singer, a memento received when they had been in a musical together. It was beautiful— personally autographed by the singer and full of sentimental value. Our hostess literally talked for three or four minutes about how meaningful the piece was to her.

No sooner did she finish talking about its significance than our dear one-year-old picked it up and dropped it on the coffee table, shattering it into a million pieces of glass. As if that wasn't enough, the water from the snow globe spilled all over the family heirloom Bible. It was one of those moments when Emily and I just looked at each other in stunned disbelief. What do you say in that kind of moment? I was very touched that our hostess responded with extraordinary grace and kindness.

This is what authentic Christian community looks like. (In fact, what happens right *after* such an incident *also* tells you what Christian community looks like). It's often messy. It's broken. It can be the equivalent of a shattered cherished snow globe in the middle of the room, which cannot be ignored.

Memories like that make me thankful for the apostle Paul's guidance about life together in community.

How Christians Grow IN COMMUNITY

In Colossians 3, Paul speaks to the Colossians Christians at length about godly behavior that flows out of the implications of the gospel. A Christian is someone who has been united to Christ in his death to sin and also in his resurrection to a new life here and now (Colossians 3:1-4). This gospel transformation, experienced by faith, is then to work itself out in a changed life. At first, he talks about what they need to *put off* (get rid of), now that they are Christ followers. Then, in verse 12, he pivots and says, *"**Put on,** then, as God's chosen ones, holy and beloved"* and he launches into a primer on what their new life in Christ should look like.

"Put on" Christian Virtues

It begins, Paul says, with a change of attitude toward others. The qualities he mentions are not simply traits we can stir up from nowhere. They must flow from a heart being *shaped* by the gospel. The qualities he lists in Colossians 3:13-16 are challenging. After all, it's a big deal to be God's chosen people. And God desires to see the work he's doing in our hearts actually manifested in the way we treat others.

Notice in Paul's list that even though each of these characteristics requires inner change (which can take place anywhere), the only place you can actually see these qualities active in a person's life is *in community* with others.

Christian character is formed in relationships.

As we review Paul's list of virtues, ask yourself, "Is this quality increasing in my life?"

Compassionate Hearts

This speaks of the heart qualities of tenderness, sympathy, understanding, and appropriate actions to accompany those feelings. When do we have the chance to *put on* compassionate hearts? When we're with people who are broken, people in need, those who are hurting or struggling. Who do you know right now in your circle of influence who could use some compassion today?

Kindness

This speaks of warmth, affection, and helpfulness. Paul is not telling us to be kind only toward people we like. Who needs to be told to be kind to people they like? He's talking about showing kindness toward people who are rude, disrespectful, late to the meeting, people who talk out of turn and who one-up all your stories. Do you know people like that? Consider it an opportunity to grow in kindness.

Humility

This is not thinking less of yourself, but, rather, thinking of yourself less. It means being honest with others about both your strengths and weaknesses, rather than maintaining a façade. It means dropping the mask and being authentic. Humility grows when you express your needs and let others help you. It's also when convicted by God's Word, you confess sin and seek the forgiveness of those your words or actions may have harmed.

Meekness/Gentleness

When gentleness grows in you, then, when you have good reason to lash out or to correct someone harshly, you choose to do it gently instead, so as not to crush his or her spirit. When you have a gentle spirit and sin is exposed in another person, you choose to find ways to build up that hurting person, rather than tear them down. Gentleness flows from humility.

Patience

Patience develops as we wait for the Word of God to do its work in others and ourselves, without impatiently trying to become the Holy Spirit for someone else. The more we truly know ourselves and our shortcomings, the more patient we become with others.

Bearing With One Another

This is a tough one. It literally means *enduring* one another. The whole idea of Christian community sounds great at first. Then we realize it means living in relationship not just with people we enjoy, but also with people we have to endure. It's being in relationship with people we can't stand, people who get on our nerves, people we wish would go away.

Furthermore, Paul *doesn't* say, "If you have in your community the kind of people you have to endure, then you must be in the wrong place. Look for a new community!" Rather, he says, "If you have these kinds of people in your community, welcome to the church!"

Of course, there's a place for boundaries. Of course, there's a place for correction, rebuke, and so on, as we'll see. But it doesn't cancel our obligation to endure one another or treat others with anything less than the other characteristics we've seen described.

Too often what we do is *avoid* such people, get upset with them, try to force them out, lash out, and then sometimes, after all that, we confront, rebuke, and exhort them! It's no wonder it doesn't work.

More growth needed up ahead! And church (our spiritual community) is the ideal place for this kind of transformation to happen.

Forgiving Each Other

To forgive is to refuse to make people pay what they owe you. Paul's not talking about a situation of perceived injustices. He's talking about forgiving *real* injustices! Someone has genuinely hurt you. You've really been wronged. Even so, it's not the time to flee community. It's the time to grow, through the application of the gospel to your real-life situation.

We never quite seem ready for that kind of real-life test of our spiritual maturity, do we? We can read over and over about forgiveness. Then, suddenly, when we're wronged, everything we read goes right out the window. Surely, we think, it doesn't apply in *this* case. I know the feeling. But Paul teaches us that a major place of growth is where we learn to forgive the people who have wronged us.

*   *   *

All the virtues we've discussed are ways that God has already acted toward *us*. So, now, because we are his people, he calls us to act the same way toward each other. **The virtues all boil down to putting the interests of others ahead of own**—the very definition of love.

"Above all, put on love"

In the end, love is the glue that holds community together and helps it thrive. Needy people, harsh people, selfish people, and boastful people—we think *they* are what keep us from being compassionate, kind, humble, gentle and forgiving. If only we were just surrounded by different people, we say. People less messy, less broken. Then we could easily exhibit all these virtues, right? Actually, it is precisely because these people are in your life that you have the opportunity to *put on* these characteristics every day. **Think of living in community as God's learning lab for our spiritual good.**

It's also important to note that Christian community doesn't just mean meekly enduring bad behavior or even maltreatment from brothers and sisters in Christ. It also includes offering positive encouragements to one another as together we grow and are transformed by Christ.

"Teaching and admonishing one another"

Both teaching and admonishing (counseling or advising) are to be done in the context of the mutual trust, forgiveness, kindness, and gentleness we've already described. It's a serious responsibility.

No, this doesn't mean we're all teachers in the formal literal sense. But it suggests each of us should be willing to share, instruct, and pass along what we've learned, as we're able. We need each other! It may be as simple as sharing in a small group or in our family what we've learned in our own reading of the God's Word, rather than being a passive listener who feels no responsibility to add to a discussion.

Admonishing also speaks of correction. There are occasional moments where a sharp rebuke is necessary, but it's rare. In 2 Timothy 2:24-25, the apostle Paul told Timothy, whom he was mentoring, that even with regard to enemies of the gospel, great self-control was appropriate. *"And the Lord's servant must not be quarrelsome but kind to everyone, able to teach, patiently enduring evil, correcting his opponents with gentleness. God may perhaps grant them repentance."*

Harshness seldom leads people to repent. That's the work of God himself. Paul suggests there is a higher likelihood of a person coming to a place of repentance through your gentleness more than through your harshness.

Paul addresses a similar situation in Galatians, where he suggests how to deal with a brother or sister who is caught in sin: *"If anyone is caught in any transgression, you who are spiritual should restore him in a spirit of gentleness."* (Galatians 6:1)

If this is true in the family life of the church, how much more should it be the case in the life of our own families? True, we who are parents have a responsibility to correct our children, to discipline and train them. But is there ever a time it should occur harshly? Even in our correction, shouldn't our actions always be characterized by gentleness?

* * *

All these scriptures confirm that living in genuine Christian community is *messy* but absolutely *necessary* for growth. Here's an interesting footnote to all this. Have you ever thought about how God works the same way in the natural world?

Think about it. What gets spread as fertilizer over the top of fields to produce maximum growth? You don't even have to say it; you can smell it! Yet, amazingly, in God's perfect economy, some of the most precious, beautiful, and nourishing produce grows from that hot smelly mess of nastiness!

The same thing happens *in community*. Precious, beautiful, nourishing growth happens in the midst of authentic, messy, relationships.

How Christians Grow THROUGH THE WORD

Look again at Colossians 3:16. Paul says, *"Let the word of Christ dwell in you richly, teaching and admonishing one another in all wisdom, singing psalms and hymns and spiritual songs, with thankfulness in your hearts to God."* Here Paul raises the value of God's Word as a tool for helping us grow.

"Let the word of Christ dwell in you richly"

We believe the Holy Spirit inspired the whole Bible. Therefore, we grow when we let scripture take up residence in our life—not just the words Christ spoke, but also the words spoken *about* him. Paul says, "Soak it up! Let the Word of God in general and the words of Christ, in particular, be at home in you. Let the Word dwell in you richly. Not meagerly. Abundantly!" Does God's Word live in you meagerly or abundantly?

Why would Paul make such a big deal about getting the Word into our lives and letting it dwell there? So we can check off a box on our spiritual disciplines checklist? No. He urges it because when God's Word is allowed to work in our lives with the help of the Holy Spirit, it changes us. It's a simple cause and effect.

**You must be a person who dwells *in* the Word,
if you want to be changed *by* the Word.**

We're to read it. Listen to it. Memorize it. Study it. Speak it. Meditate on it.

I was recently reminded how powerful it can be to just plain read God's Word, pure and unadulterated. I read a lot of books. At any given time, I have a book lying open on most flat surfaces in our home, so that no matter where I am I have something to read.

However, on a recent trip to India, I decided I was just going to read God's Word. I didn't take any other books.

Since my sleep schedule was off due to the change in time zones, I had opportunity to soak in the Word for hours at a time. On a couple of occasions, I put on headphones and listened to the reading of Scripture as I fell asleep. On another occasion, I sat and listened to the entire book of Hebrews read aloud. The effect was amazing. The more I took in, the hungrier for the Word I became.

Some of you may not feel comfortable "dwelling" in God's Word. You may feel you don't understand what it says, so you're afraid to take a deep dive. Or maybe you say, "I just don't enjoy reading it."

One of my heroes of the faith, George Muller, has some excellent advice. Muller was an 18th Century British evangelist who started 117 schools and provided a Christian education to 120,000 children, mostly orphans:

> If the reader understands very little of the Word of God, he ought to read it very much; for the Spirit explains the Word by the Word. And if he enjoys the reading of the Word little, that is just the reason why he should read it much; for the frequent reading of the Scriptures creates a delight in them, so that the more we read them, the more we desire to do so.[1]

That's my experience. Frequent reading of the Word not only increases our understanding, but it can also create an insatiable hunger and thirst for it.

Obstacles to Growing through the Word

It's naïve to suggest that letting the Word dwell in us richly is a simple task. For one thing, who has the time? And what about all our unanswered questions? Satan knows these are real issues and uses them as speed bumps to dissuade any enthusiasm for growth in this area.

J.I. Packer writes, "If I were the devil, one of my first aims would be to stop folks from digging into the Bible. Knowing that it is the Word of God, teaching men to know and love and serve the God of the Word, I should do all I could to surround it with the spiritual equivalent of pits, thorn hedges, and man traps, to frighten people off."[2] Isn't that how it feels sometimes? You reach for the Bible and suddenly a hundred other things seem more pressing?

But here's a stunning fact. I did a little research and learned that a person can actually read the entire Bible—out loud at pulpit rate—in somewhere between 69 and 77 hours.[3] That's still a sizeable chunk of time, but let's put it in perspective. According to a Nielsen survey, the average American watches five hours of television per day.[4] That works out to 35 hours per week. In other words, if you're an average American, you could read the whole Bible in two weeks simply by replacing TV watching with Bible reading.

And, if you think those statistics apply only to young people, the same Nielsen survey found that people over 50 watch the most TV of all age groups—approximately 50 hours per week! That's over 7 hours per day. At that rate, you could read the Bible cover-to-cover in 10 days! And that doesn't even include the time spent on social media.

I'm not suggesting that you eliminate TV or social media. But somewhere in your day I suspect each of you could carve out some amount of regular time to *dwell* in the Word for the sake of your spiritual growth. The question is: How hungry are you to grow?

I read the story of a man in Kansas City who was severely injured in an explosion that messed up his face, destroyed his eyesight and took his hands. Apparently, the man had become a

Christian shortly before the accident, so one of his greatest disappointments was not being able to read the Bible.

He heard about a lady in England who read Braille with her lips, so he ordered the Bible in Braille. Unfortunately, his lips were too damaged to distinguish between the Braille dots. But as he brought one of the Braille pages to his lips, his tongue happened to touch a few of the raised characters and he could feel them. At the time the book about him was written, he had already read through the Bible four times *with his tongue.*[5]

How far will you go to dwell in the Word and to let it dwell in you? Pray for that kind of hunger and then dwell *in the Word* until the hunger comes.

How Christians Grow BY THE SPIRIT

So far, we've seen how spiritual growth happens *in community,* as we put on Christ-like virtues and teach and admonish one another. We've also seen how growth happens when we're *in the Word,* letting it dwell in us richly. But, honestly, even though we can create an environment for growth, it isn't something we can manufacture entirely on our own. Think of the farmer who creates all the right conditions for growth, but he can't actually make corn pop up from the soil.

In 1 Corinthians 3:5-7, Paul explains how divine help is needed for optimal growth: *"What, then, is Apollos? What is Paul? Servants, through whom you believed as the Lord assigned to each. I planted, Apollos watered, but God gave the growth. So neither he who plants nor he who waters is anything, but only God who gives the growth."*

Clearly, Paul says, we do our part, God's Word does its part, but then God, who works in us *through the Holy Spirit*, gives the growth.

**It is the *Spirit* of God working
through the *Word* of God in the *community* of God
that promotes the *growth* of God's people.**

So here's my challenge to you—an action plan to give you breakthrough to a deeper, more satisfying relationship with the Lord and our faith community.

STEP 1: Commit Yourself to the Word

Commit to a daily and consistent time to read the Word of God. I'm not going to prescribe where or how much time to spend. That's between you and God. *You* determine what it will take to let the word of Christ dwell in you *richly*.

To help you focus, you may want to select some kind of a Bible reading plan. For those of you who like to read on your phone, the YouVersion Bible app (*www.youversion.com*) has an enormous variety of reading plans, in addition to several translations of the Bible. I personally don't like to read the Bible on my phone, but through the YouVersion app I can plug headphones in and listen to *audio* readings of any part of the Bible I select, which is very helpful.

For a reading plan that is accompanied by a series of excellent animated videos that introduce each book of the Bible and explain important biblical themes, I highly recommend The Bible Project (*www.thebibleproject.com*). Currently, our church is using The Bible Project videos, along with an app called Read Scripture (*www.readscripture.org),* to read through the Bible together as a community this year. If, like me, you prefer to read the Bible straight out of the printed Word, we have printed copies available of our Read Scripture plan.

Finally, any major online Christian portal will have more plans. For example, Ligonier Ministries has a variety of reading plans at *https://www.ligonier.org/blog/bible-reading-plans/*. Honestly, it doesn't matter which one you choose. Just choose one and do your best to be intentional about it every day.

STEP 2: Commit Yourself to Community Around the Word

As we've already said, the value of reading the Word on your own is immense. But apart from a real community in which to live it out, you are depriving yourself of one of God's divinely appointed means of growth. You need to be involved in a group small enough where you can know and be known by others. That's where we'll have opportunity to *put on* compassion, kindness, humility, gentleness, patience, and so on.

Here are a few options for you to check out at Covenant:

Adult Fellowship Communities (which we call AFC)

These meet every Sunday morning at the same time, before or after whichever service you attend, with a variety of topics to choose from. You can check out the topics online at our website *(www.covenantnaples.com)* or pick up a copy of the *Covenant Monthly* at the Welcome Desk in the foyer. It's an easy place to get connected because you'll already be at church. These are typically Bible studies without time for deep fellowship. But it's a way to get to know a few people better, which is why it's important to commit to attending regularly in order to gain the full benefit.

Midweek Connection

On Wednesday nights we have a lineup of classes in a smaller setting, to allow more interaction around God's Word. A roster of current offerings is available at the Welcome Desk, through the

Covenant Monthly or online. These are typically four-to-eight-week classes on a variety of topics—from straight Bible studies to studies that offer instruction from a biblical perspective on practical life issues like how to grow healthier marriages or biblical parenting or financial freedom.

Small Groups

Small groups are a wonderful way not only to gather with others around God's Word, but also to share what's going on in your life, form deep relationships, and gain support and encouragement. Some groups are coed, some not. Some are a mix of singles and couples, some are just couples. Some meet in homes and others meet at church on a day and time of the group's choosing. It is community at its best. The Welcome Desk can give you the name of someone who can help you get connected to a group.

Midsize Groups

Both Covenant's men's and women's ministries hold weekly gatherings—both morning and evening opportunities—around a short teaching and breakout discussion groups on a variety of topics which change every few weeks. Again, the emphasis is on building community around the Word, with an emphasis on learning how God's Word applies to our daily lives.

*　　*　　*

I agree with N.T. Wright who wrote, "The church is to be as stocked with good teaching as a palace is filled with treasures."[6]

We don't expect you to show up at church every time the doors are open. However, it's our deep desire that all of you are in at least one community group on a regular basis, where you are dwelling *in the Word* together.

Admittedly, some of these groups aren't small enough to allow enough time for the deeper relationship building like we're talking about. But, by being a part of one of these larger communities, you can often find two or three other people that you can start meeting with on a regular basis to develop stronger connections with each other around God's Word.

I've recently just started meeting with two other Christian men on a weekly basis and we keep each other accountable for reading the Word and doing what it says.

Furthermore, as I've said before, for those of you with a family, you already have a divinely appointed small group. Don't miss the opportunity to regularly dwell in the Word together with your family

I hope by now you are firmly convinced that we are a church committed to the Word because we believe, by the Spirit's power, God uses it to grow us to be more like Christ.

In their book, *The Trellis and the Vine,* Colin Marshall and Tony Payne describe my vision for our church:

> Imagine if all Christians, as a normal part of their discipleship, were caught up in a web of regular Bible reading—not only digging into the Word privately, but reading it with their children before bed, with their spouse over breakfast, with a non-Christian colleague at work once a week over lunch, with a new Christian for follow-up once a fortnight for mutual encouragement, and with a mature Christian friend once a month for mutual encouragement. It would be a chaotic web of personal relationships, prayer, and Bible reading—more of a movement than a program.[7]

Does that ignite your heart and whet your appetite for what's possible? Let's commit together, as God's chosen and beloved children, to that kind of holy momentum. May it accelerate making our own Covenant Mission Statement a reality:

**We will develop and deploy
fully devoted followers of Jesus Christ,
to disciple our family, community, and world.**

BETWEEN YOU AND GOD

1. What's the hardest part for you, when it comes to building community with other Christians? What would others say is the hardest part about being in community with *you*? Talk about it with God.

2. Which of the Christian virtues listed in this chapter do you feel are your strengths? Which ones do you believe you need to work on? List them and use a concordance to look for Scriptures that talk about these virtues.

3. If you are not already plugged into some kind of community group, review some of the options available and commit to getting involved. We need each other.

---

[1] George Muller, *A Narrative of Some of the Lord's Dealings with George Muller*, Eighth Edition (London, J. Nisbet & Co., 1881), 30.
[2] J.I. Packer, Foreword, R.C. Sproul, *Knowing Scripture* Revised Edition, (InterVarsity Press, 2009), 9.
[3] *http://www.euxton.com/bible.htm* calculates it at 70 hours and 40 minutes.
[4] John Koblin, *https://www.nytimes.com/2016/07/01/business/media/nielsen-survey-media-viewing.html.*
[5] Donald Whitney, *Spiritual Disciplines for the Christian Life* (NavPress, 1991), 35.
[6] N.T. Wright, *Colossians and Philemon, Tyndale New Testament Commentary* (Eerdmans Publishing Co., 2002), 144.
[7] Colin Marshall and Tony Payne, *The Trellis and the Vine, The Ministry Mind-Shift That Changes Everything* (Matthias Media, 2009), 57.

Chapter 5

GROW

In Grace and Knowledge

I learned a few interesting things while teaching our three kids how to ride a bike. First, on a purely practical level, I learned I needed to stretch before beginning the lesson. The combination of running short choppy steps, while bending over supporting a child in front of me, doesn't agree with my back or hamstrings! Second, helmets and pads are a good idea, for obvious reasons. And third, the key to success is not teaching the child to balance, but rather teaching them to pedal and keep themselves moving forward. Balance comes automatically with forward motion. But when they stop pedaling, they stop moving and they fall. Every time.

Living the Christian life can be like riding a bike. As long as we keep pedaling and moving forward, we can always make adjustments to our balance. But once we stop making forward progress, we fall.

Why is it that some of us stop moving forward in the Christian life? Why do we stop growing?

- **We think we've "arrived."** We don't think we need to grow anymore. We think we've pretty much figured out how the Christian life works. Both Peter and Paul repeatedly debunked that myth in Scripture (check out Philippians 3:8-16 and 2 Peter 1:3-10), urging believers to keep going and making clear that none of us have "arrived."

- **We have a besetting sin in our life that keeps beating us down.** In other words, a sin, a struggle, or difficulty that continues to harass us. For example, think of a critical parent or spouse who relentlessly berates their loved ones for seemingly doing everything wrong. They know they need to get a handle on their critical spirit but can't seem to shake it. They may have made some effort to act differently, but see little evidence of lasting change, so they simply give up. I get it. There's nothing worse than pedaling, only to feel like you're rolling backward down the hill

- **We're distracted.** We start out pedaling strong, but all the shiny things around us capture our attention and we forget what's important.

Can you relate to any of these growth interrupters? If you have a personal relationship with Jesus Christ, here's a truth that should encourage you to press on and not give up on spiritual growth:

**In him you already have *everything* you need
to grow to full maturity.**

When you put your trust in Christ and began a new relationship with him, your faith unleashed the power of God in your life to bring about growth and transformation. Of course, that's not the whole story. God likes to do things together *with* us. So, while he does *his* part, *we* have a role to play, too.

In 2 Peter 1:5-8 we're told, *"Make every effort to supplement your faith with virtue, and virtue with knowledge, and knowledge with self-control, and self-control with steadfastness, and steadfastness with godliness, and godliness with brotherly affection, and brotherly affection with love. For if these qualities are yours and are increasing, they keep you from being ineffective or unfruitful in the knowledge of our Lord Jesus Christ."*

Peter is saying, "Okay, now that you have this faith-based relationship with God, the way to *keep growing* is to keep pursuing by faith the qualities that make us more like Jesus. Make them a habit. (Keep pedaling!) You'll grow."

There are good reasons why Scripture keeps hammering home the idea to grow, grow, grow:

We're to Grow Because of What's Coming

When Jesus returns, two life-altering events will happen—things that will make you glad you pursued spiritual maturity:

The Judgment of God

Jesus will come suddenly and without warning to usher in a time of judgment. There will be no place to hide. Every one of us will have our actions examined and our hearts and thoughts exposed.

It will be a terrifying and devastating time for those who have not made peace with God, because, at that point, there will be no opportunity to make that choice. Jesus will be about the business of settling accounts and restoring God's creation to what he originally intended before mankind's sin messed up his plans for this world and the people in it.

Authors Dick Lucas and Christopher Green, in their commentary on 2 Peter, say, "Only those who are striving after holiness would dare to wish for the coming of the Day of the Lord."[1]

For Christians, Jesus' return will be a great and glorious day! We will finally see our Savior face-to-face and he will usher in a restoration project like the world has never seen.

Nevertheless, God doesn't want anyone to perish. In 2 Peter 3:9, we learn that God is holding off Jesus' return to give more time to those who have not yet decided to repent and believe the gospel. *"The Lord is not slow to fulfill his promise as some count slowness, but is patient toward you, not wishing that any should perish, but that all should reach repentance."* However, don't miss the implication here: some *are* perishing and some *will* perish when he returns. It's a sobering thought.

Until then, the action step for believers is to pursue lives of godliness and holiness. The action step for *un*believers is to repent (renounce their sin) and place their trust in Jesus. The stakes are high. Not one of us will stand before God and rely on our own goodness at The Judgment.

The New Heavens and New Earth

After The Judgment comes the prize. Peter says, *"But, according to his promise, we are waiting for new heavens and a new earth in which righteousness dwells."* (2 Peter 3:13) The word used for heaven here is plural, to communicate to the ancient mind that God's entire universe will get a makeover—the sun, the moon, and stars, along with what we traditionally think of as the *place* called heaven.

This is not heaven as we often picture it—an ethereal place with elevator music and extremely bright lights, where we float around as disembodied souls for eternity. This is *a new creation* that will emerge after God has cleansed the world of sin and its effects and forever set it free from the bondage of decay.

One author described it this way: "Sin, which has marred God's world, will not be permitted to have the final word. In a renewed universe, the ravages of the fall will be repaired by the glory of the restoration. Paradise Lost will become Paradise Regained."[2]

You may be thinking, "Why, then, do I have to work on my spiritual growth, since God is going to make everything perfect, anyway, with this 'new creation'?"

I'm glad you asked. Besides the fact that becoming more like Christ is our great joy and brings glory to God, God wants us to give our culture a *current* picture of what humanity will look like in the *future* world of righteousness. It's like saying, "World, look at us and catch a glimpse of what God wants to do in us and with us when he returns." The only way we'll be able to fulfill that assignment is if we *grow in grace and knowledge.*

How will we know we're growing? We'll look more and more like Jesus. We'll show more love, more grace. There will be more distinctiveness between us and the world, more submission, more fruitfulness, more joy, more peace, and, yes, there will likely be more suffering and persecution in the process.

Here's the point. God didn't give us information about Christ's second coming—The Judgment and the new heavens and new earth—just to *inform* us, as in, "Write this down, so you won't be surprised." Rather, the knowledge of his return is supposed to produce a response in us.

A.W. Tozer says, "No man is better for knowing that God, in the beginning, created the heaven and the earth. The devil knows that, and so did Ahab and Judas Iscariot. No man is better for knowing that God so loved the world of men that He gave his only begotten Son to die for their redemption. In hell, there are millions who know that. **Theological truth is useless until it is obeyed.**

The purpose behind all doctrine is to secure moral action."[3] [Emphasis added]

So, how do you measure up to Tozer's definition of discipleship? Are you taking action, pedaling with enthusiasm, and looking forward to the new heavens and new earth? Or is there a broken link between your beliefs and your behavior? Does your present life reflect the hope of the world to come or is your hope more earthbound?

Don't feel discouraged if you're not where you want to be or where you know God wants you to be. Every day we have a new opportunity to resist our preoccupation with this temporary life and commit to growing in grace and knowledge, because of the magnificent future that's coming.

We're to Grow Because There's Work to Do Before He Comes

Assignment #1: Make Disciples

I think most Christians would agree that to grow in grace and knowledge is noble, important, and God honoring. But when we continue to grow in knowledge without obedience or sharing what we've learned with others, we quench the flow of the Holy Spirit in our lives.

A now-exiled Chinese evangelist, known as Brother Yun, has led countless people to Christ. He was instrumental in the development of Christian house church networks in China during the 1980s and 90s. He offers a compelling insight into what's lacking in churches in the West and how we can be more fruitful:

> The answer to experiencing God's living water is not to seek more and more Bible teaching. The answer is not to attend more Christian conferences or seek new ministers

with new messages. ... The key for experiencing the flow of God's living water in your life is obedience. Most Christians I have met in the Western world have plenty of Bible knowledge, but they do not experience the living water flowing from their lives because of their disobedience. **God doesn't want you to know everything and do nothing. He would rather you know a little and act on that little, in obedience, and then he will give you more.**[4] [Emphasis added]

He's right. There's nothing wrong with Bible knowledge; we need it. There's nothing wrong with conferences. But if we're not seeing God powerfully at work in our lives, it may *not* be because we lack enough Bible knowledge. It may be because we're not obeying what we already know.

We know that God went to extraordinary lengths to restore his relationship with his children—a relationship broken by our sin. And we know he wants us to reach out to those who are far from him, to share the Good News and bring others into the family as disciples, too. So what are we waiting for?

We don't grow first, then go.
We don't wait until we're "ready."
We grow in grace and knowledge
and
we go and make disciples
at the same time.

Assignment #2: Watch Out for Errors

In 2 Peter 3:16, Peter describes how some of the people were distorting Scripture written by Paul. It's easy to do because not everything Paul wrote was simple to understand. Look at verse 16, *"There are some things in them that are hard to understand, which the ignorant and unstable twist to their own destruction, as they do the other Scriptures."*

Peter is warning us that there will always be ignorant and unstable people who distort God's Word to their own destruction, not to mention the harm it brings to others in the church. Their false teaching was no small thing. They removed the need for the gospel and salvation altogether, which is the very foundation of our faith.

False teachers were telling people that once a person was justified (declared righteous by God's grace), they could do whatever they wanted with total impunity. In fact, some were even saying you should sin all you wanted, so grace could abound more!

Today, people continue to twist the message of Scripture, particularly in order to allow immorality. Why else would we see Christian churches condoning sexual liberties that the Bible itself says lead to destruction? Or churches condoning greed or condoning a lack of compassion for marginalized people?

So Peter warns them (and us) in verse 17, *"You, therefore, beloved, knowing this beforehand, take care that you are not carried away with the error of lawless people and lose your own stability."* It's apparent that people to whom he's writing are experienced and well instructed. They stand on stable ground, but Peter doesn't want them duped into losing that sound footing.

Is there a shortcut to that kind of stability? I don't think so.

**Diligent study of the Word will always be
an important part of our Christian life.**

What we need to know in order to be saved is relatively simple to grasp. But there will often be other things about our faith that are harder to understand. We must press on to maturity, so we won't be easily derailed.

Think again of the bike illustration. If we're moving forward and we keep pedaling (keep growing), we're far less susceptible to be carried away by distorted theology. Or, in the words of New Testament scholar Gene Green, "The best antidote against apostasy [abandonment of a religious belief] is a Christian life that is growing."[5]

*   *   *

We've talked about *growing in knowledge*—that deepening of our understanding of the truth of Christ, a deepening that should increase until we see Jesus face-to-face. But what does it mean to *grow in grace*?

It is to know, increasingly at the core of your being, that you are loved, you are accepted, and you are the object of God's delight, purely because of his unmerited favor lavished on you. A person *growing in grace* is increasingly gentle with others, increasingly humble, increasingly forgiving, increasingly compassionate, and increasingly loving. That person increasingly hates sin and loves what is good.

**Growing in both knowledge *and* grace is a
powerful safeguard against heresy and apostasy.**

Here are a couple of the most common errors to watch out for:

Error #1   **"Knowledge doesn't matter, only grace."**

In Paul's day, people were saying things like, "We should sin more, so that grace abounds!" Today you'll hear people say, "How you live doesn't ultimately matter. Love wins!" Another variation of this is, "It doesn't matter what you believe, as long as you're sincere. There are many paths to God."

Sounds good, doesn't it? No judgment. Everybody's happy. Just pick some theology and believe it with all your heart. Any one will do. They're all variations on the theme that says we don't need to grow in knowledge, but only to grow in grace.

However, discernment is needed. As Peter explained in 2 Peter 3:17, *"Don't be carried away by lawless men and lose your own stability."* False teaching is contrary to the clear teaching of Scripture. So, if you want to grow in the grace and knowledge of Jesus, dwell more in the Word than in the world, so you'll be able to recognize false teaching when you hear or read it.

Error #2:   "Grace doesn't matter, only knowledge."

Like the first error, no one would use this exact phrase, but it's reflected in people's actions and attitude. It expresses itself in a lack of compassion for the poor, the victims of injustice, the woman caught in adultery, and the man with a criminal record. "They should know better," people say.

This error leaves the impression that even though you're a Christian you're still under God's condemnation. It suggests our salvation is something we maintain by our own efforts. It's easy to lean into this error if we think God only saves good people, "people like us."

This thinking has the appearance of godliness but denies God's power—to redeem the hopelessly broken, free people from addictions, heal the sick. These "only-knowledge" people are always learning, learning, learning—like the Pharisees—but never coming to a full knowledge of God's truth.

Each of us seems to have a disposition for either growing in the grace of Jesus or growing in the knowledge of Jesus. You'll know your inclination by asking which position feels more dangerous to hold.

**Whichever side you're more afraid of is probably your
weakness. Christian growth means growing in *both*
grace and knowledge.**

Those who are only interested in growing in *knowledge* end up
in dead orthodoxy, naval gazing, not caring about the world, and
not sharing their faith. Those only interested in growing in *grace*
end up in an emotional pietism, susceptible to immorality, duped
by every new theological fad, driven by feelings at the expense of
the truth.

G.K. Chesterton once wrote, "Orthodoxy is like walking along
a narrow ridge, almost like a knife-edge. One step to either side
was a step to disaster. Jesus is God and man; God is love and
holiness; Christianity is grace and morality; the Christian lives in
this world and in the world of eternity. Over-stress either side of
these great truths and at once destructive heresy emerges."[6]

As Christians, God calls us to grow in both knowledge *and*
grace because it will help balance life between the two
extremes—the two ditches on either side of the road.

*   *   *

We've now covered two of the four Rhythms of Discipleship:
Worship and Grow. Are you beginning to see how a committed
life of discipleship helps us fulfill the important mission the Lord
has given us?

If we are to be effective for the kingdom:

- We must respond to the gospel by cultivating a life of
  worship in the sanctuary, in the living room, and in the
  closet—making our whole life an expression of worship.

- Individually and collectively, we must continue to **grow** in the grace and knowledge of Jesus Christ by the Spirit's power, working through the Word, in community.

- We must respond to the gospel by **serving** one another with our time, talents, and treasure, leveraging everything God has given us for the sake of his Kingdom.

- We must respond to the gospel by intentionally **going** to our family, community, and world every day, proclaiming good news and doing good works in Jesus's name.

If we live this rhythm with passion and commitment, we will fulfill our mission:

To develop and deploy
fully devoted followers of Jesus Christ,
to disciple our family, community, and world.

Jesus is coming again! Until that day, he invites us to get our own lives and the world around us ready for his glorious return. It will be more satisfying than any other assignment you've ever had.

BETWEEN YOU AND GOD

1. Do you live your life in *anticipation* of the Day of Judgment or in *fear* of it? What changes would you like to make in your life to live more intentionally from an eternal perspective?

2. Do you feel you give the world around you a good picture of what a person looks like who's being transformed by God? What needs to change?

3. Do you feel you lean too far toward believing that being right is more important than being gracious? Or do you believe that being gracious is more important than being right? Ask God to make you more aware when you are out of balance.

---

[1]Dick Lucas and Christopher Green, *The Message of 2 Peter and Jude* (InterVarsity Press, 1995), 146.
[2] Michael Green, *2 Peter and Jude, Tyndale New Testament Commentary* (IVP Academic, 2009), 165.
[3]A.W. Tozer, *The Best of A.W. Tozer* (compiled by Warren Wiersbe, Baker Book House, 1978), 140-141.
[4]Brother Yun, *Living Water* (Zondervan, 2008), 116-117.
[5]Gene Green, *Jude and 2 Peter, Baker Exegetical Commentary of the New Testament* (Baker Academic, 2008), 343.
[6] G. K. Chesterton, quoted by Michael Green, *2 Peter and Jude, Tyndale New Testament Commentary*, (IVP Academic, 2009), 171.

Chapter 6

SERVE

Understanding and Using Our Spiritual Gifts

By Todd Augustine

In his book *Has Christianity Failed You?* Ravi Zacharias points to one of the greatest proofs for the truth of Christ and the reality of the resurrection. It's the changed lives of Christians. Zacharias writes:

> During the course of nearly 40 years, I have traveled to virtually every continent and seen or heard some of the most amazing testimonies of God's intervention in the most extreme circumstances. I have seen hardened criminals touched by the message of Jesus Christ and their hearts turned toward good in a way that no rehabilitation could have accomplished. I have seen ardent followers of radical belief systems turned from being violent, brutal terrorists to becoming mild, tenderhearted followers of Jesus Christ. I have seen nations where the gospel—banned and silenced by governments—has nevertheless conquered the ethos and mindset of an entire culture.[1]

Then Zacharias gives this example of Christ's power to transform lives:

In the middle of the twentieth century, after destroying all of the Christian seminary libraries in the country [China], Chairman Mao declared that the last vestiges of Christianity had been permanently removed from China, never to make a return. On Easter Sunday in 2009, close to half a century later, the leading English-language newspaper in Hong Kong published a picture of Tiananmen Square with Jesus replacing the picture of Chairman Mao's picture on a gigantic banner and the words 'Christ is Risen' [raised up for all to see].[2]

That's a picture of the radical nature of Christianity—able to turn entire cultures inside out and upside down, because of the ability of the gospel to penetrate the human heart and bring radical transformation. That's also a glorious picture of the church when it's at work in the world, spreading the gospel and changing lives. It's the same church described in Acts 17:6—*"men who have turned the world upside down."*

Where is that church today? As you look across our land, is that the church you see? Do you see a church shaping and *changing* culture or is it a church that has been shaped and changed *by* its culture? Or, even more disappointing, is it a church that's become dull, numb, lacking any sense of urgency, unable to change the world in which it exists.

How about us? Where do you think Covenant falls on the spiritual passion spectrum? What kind of church are *we*? Could it be said of us, "Look at these men/women/children who have turned the world upside down!" Do we share that same *radical* nature? That same *sense of urgency*? That *same sense of purpose*? Are we *changing* the world around us or are we being changed *by* it?

That is precisely what Peter had in mind when he penned 1 Peter to the First Century Church. Simply stated, Peter envisioned a church that was *captivated by the cross, motivated by love* and *animated by grace.* In this picture of the church, Peter shows what it means for the church to *serve.*

Serve is the third discipline in our Rhythm of Discipleship (Worship, Grow, **Serve**, Go). It's the logical time to talk about spiritual gifts since God gave us these gifts to *serve* the church and the world. But, first, let's look at the context in which those gifts are exercised.

Peter paints for us a picture of the New Testament church. But before he calls believers to serve, he shows what the community was about, what moves them and enables them to serve. In his view, there were three essentials that enabled genuine serving to happen in the church.

The Serving Church is a Cross-Captivated Church

We often hear the term "cross-cultural" used today. When used in reference to the church, it means a diverse church of many cultures, ethnicities, and backgrounds, which is a good thing. However, the apostle Peter described the New Testament church as a *cross-captivated* church—where the cross drove the culture of the church. The cross was at its center. Let me explain.

In 1 Peter 4:7, Peter writes, *"The end of all things is at hand; therefore, be self-controlled and sober-minded for the sake of your prayers."*

When Peter speaks of "the end of all things" he is not talking literally about the end of the world. If he was, then he is at least two thousand years off the mark. Rather, he is speaking about the *purpose* of all things, the achievement of all things, the goal, the carrying out of all things, the fulfillment of God's redemptive plan that culminates in the life, death and resurrection of his Son, which will be brought to completion when Christ returns in all his glory.

Let me connect for you the great gospel truth of 1 Peter 3:18 to what Peter wrote in 1 Peter 4:7. Peter says: *"For Christ also suffered once for sins, the righteous for the unrighteous, that he might bring us to God, being put to death in the flesh, but made alive in the spirit."*

The plan that God put in place before the foundation of the world came to its fulfillment in Christ. Who is this Christ? He is the Anointed One, the Promised One of Genesis 3:15, the One who would crush the head of the serpent [Satan] and conquer sin and death forever. That is the gospel in full color.

Jesus died on the cross for you. He took your sins upon himself. He bore the punishment you deserved. He suffered in your place. But, as John Stott writes in his book *The Cross of Christ*, "Before we can begin to see the cross as something done *for* us, we have to see it as something done *by* us." [Emphasis added] *I* put Jesus on the cross; my sin put him there. *You* put him there; your sin put him there. For all sin is an infinite offense against a holy God.

Jesus did everything that was needed to bring you to God, the only thing you must do is believe in him, trust him, put your faith in him for the forgiveness of sin and cleansing from all unrighteousness.

Stott continues, "It was by his [Christ's] death that he wished above all else to be remembered. There is, then, it is safe to say, no Christianity without the cross. If the cross is not central to our religion, ours is not the religion of Jesus."

This is what it means to be *captivated by the cross*—to be looking to the cross every day for life, purpose, and meaning. It is why, as referenced earlier, Peter says, *"Be self-controlled and sober-minded"* for the sake of your prayers, for the sake of your relationship with God. Be focused, sensible, and reasonable, in your right mind. Be in control of your thoughts.

How do you do that? What should you be thinking about? Peter tells us earlier in 1 Peter 1:13, when he uses the exact same wording: *"Therefore, preparing your minds for action, and being* *sober-minded, **set your hope fully on the grace that [comes to you in Christ].*** [Emphasis added]

The sober-minded, self-controlled person is focused on the cross because it shows the beauty of Christ, the One who died to bring you to God! This, Peter says, should power your prayer life. It should further your love for God and deepen your relationship with him. Since the end of all things is at hand, it should move you to action.

There's an urgency here. So Peter moves from talking about your prayer life to talking about your love life. He moves from how you relate to God personally, and how you must be focused on the cross, to how you relate to others.

The Serving Church is a Love-Motivated Church

Please don't miss this. When the church makes the cross the center of all things, it's not only motivated *by* love but is motivated *to* love. In 2 Cor. 5:14-15, the apostle Paul says, *"For the love of Christ controls us, because we have concluded this: that one has died for all, therefore all have died; and he died for all, that those who live might no longer live for themselves but for him who for their sake died and was raised."*

The love of Christ controls us and compels us to live no longer for ourselves but for him who died and was raised.

In a talk about spiritual gifts, Tim Keller said,

> **What it means to live a Christian life is that you put to death the right to live as you choose. You put to death the idea that you belong to yourself.** [Emphasis added] You put to death the idea that you know best what should happen in your life. You put that to death, and you give it to God. It feels like a death to really say, 'You know best, and I trust you. Here's what you say in your Word, and I don't like it, but I'm going to do it. I don't choose

anymore.' ... It feels like a death, but, on the other side, it is life.[3]

Though a relationship with God starts at the personal level, it's never supposed to remain there.

**There is no individual spirituality,
church-of-one,
I-don't-need-anybody-else,
solo Christianity
described in Scripture.**

We need each other.

We need the church because we need *one another*. Three times Peter mentions how to *relate* to one another and *love* one another. We need to be motivated by a love that is earnest, forgiving, and hospitable. *"Above all, keep loving one another earnestly, since love covers a multitude of sins. Show hospitality to one another without grumbling."* (1 Peter 4:8-9)

Let's break it down:

- **Earnest love**—is a diligent, persistent love. It means loving even when someone is curt, short, rude, and blurts out the first thing that comes to mind, without any thought about how others might hear it. Earnest love is a constant intentional love, even when faced with difficulties. If you are motivated to love *earnestly*, it means you stay the course, even when someone is hard to love. In friendships, in small groups, in marriage.

- **Forgiving love**—covers a multitude of sin, doesn't hold grudges against another person, doesn't look for retaliation when wronged. If you are learning to love one another, then you *will* eventually be hurt or offended. Love that has the cross at its center doesn't look for the exit when someone says or does something hurtful, offensive, or stupid.

- **Hospitable love**—speaks of gracious hospitality. Yes, it means having people in your home. But, even more, it speaks of "openheartedness" toward other believers and a kindness toward sojourners. And, as you love others hospitably, you do so without grumbling or complaint, but cheerfully and gladly.

Remember when Paul wrote about spiritual gifts in 1 Corinthians 13, often called the love chapter? He says, "If I can do all these things, but do not have love, then I am nothing." *Love* is at the heart of serving.

This leads us, then, to our final prerequisite for genuine service in the church.

The Serving Church is a Grace-Animated Church

To be animated is to be full of life, vigorous, lively, moved to action. An animated movie is a series of still cartoons that are set in motion. The church is always to be a moving, active, growing body of believers. What makes this possible is God's grace.

We see it in two ways. First, it shows in the way God gives gifts. *"As each has received a gift, use it to serve one another, as good stewards of God's varied grace."* (1 Peter 4:10) We all get gifts.

When the Spirit comes,
he never comes empty-handed.
God gives spiritual gifts
to each and every one of his children.

A gift is an act of grace. It is given not because it's deserved, but because of the kindness of the giver. In fact, the word for grace is *charis,* the root of the word for gift, which is *charisma.* Every good and perfect gift is from above, from God.

Spiritual gifts are a grace gift
with a particular purpose.

It's often been said that grace is the key word to understanding all of Christianity. The story is told of C.S. Lewis walking into a meeting where religious scholars from around the world were debating whether or not there was anything truly unique about Christianity. Reportedly, they turned to Lewis at one point and asked him, "What do you think?" And Lewis responded, "Oh that's an easy one. One word: grace."

Listen to what J.I. Packer says about grace:

> It thus appears that, rightly understood, this one word 'grace' contains within itself the whole of New Testament theology. The New Testament message is just the announcement that grace has come to men in and through Jesus Christ, plus a summons from God to receive this grace and to know it, and not to frustrate it, but to continue in it, since, 'the word of his grace is able to build you up, and to give you the inheritance among all those who are sanctified.' Grace is the sum and substance of New Testament faith.[4]

Since grace is at the heart of the Christian faith, it must be at the heart of this church.

If we miss grace,
if we're not a grace-saturated/grace-intoxicated people,
then we miss the whole point of the gospel.

**We undercut the very message we've been given
to proclaim to the world.**

Grace is what we were given to steward. Think of the biblical picture of Joseph, a steward given responsibility for overseeing Pharaoh's house for the good of his master. So it is with spiritual gifts. They are given for the good of the church. They are to be used for the building up of the body of Christ.

Spiritual gifts fall into two general categories: speaking gifts and serving gifts. Here's how Covenant explains spiritual gifts:

The Speaking Gifts:

- **Prophecy:** This is the forth-telling of the inspired Word of God, primarily to the body for the purpose of confirming the written Word; its purpose is to edify, exhort, and console. It can declare God's will in a particular circumstance and in some cases predict future events. Prophecy is always subject to the written Word of God and the oversight of the elders of the church.

- **Teaching**: The Spirit-given ability to faithfully and powerfully communicate the Word of God in a clear and concise way that bears fruit in the life of the hearer.

- **Exhortation**: The Spirit-given ability to effectively minister words of encouragement, consolation, comfort, and motivation.

- **Word of Knowledge:** The Spirit-given ability to speak facts or information that can only be revealed by God.

- **Word of Wisdom**: The Spirit-given ability to apply knowledge to make proper choices in difficult situations that may confound conventional wisdom.

- **Leadership**: The Spirit-given ability to influence, inspire, and mobilize people to accomplish goals for the glory of God.

- **Discernment**: The Spirit-given ability to distinguish between spirits, such as good and evil, truthful or deceiving, prophetic versus satanic.

- **Speaking in various kinds of tongues**: The Spirit-given ability to speak in an unlearned language. Speaking in tongues publicly is appropriate if it can be interpreted, so the church as a whole can be built up and if it's done in an orderly way. It is always subject to Scripture and the oversight of the elders. When a person speaks in tongues privately, it is a form of prayer or praise to God. In neither case is it to be seen as evidence of the baptism of the Holy Spirit, but rather a gracious gifting God sovereignly bestows for his own glory and the building up of believers.

- **Interpretation of Tongues**: The Spirit-given ability to interpret a message in tongues, translated into a known language, so that the hearers will be edified. It is always subject to Scripture and the oversight of the elders.

- **Evangelism**: The Spirit-given ability to share and explain the gospel message with unbelievers in such a way that there are extraordinary results in terms of conversion and discipleship.

The Serving Gifts:

- **Service/helps:** The Spirit-given ability to identify the unmet needs involved in a task related to God's work, and to make use of available resources to meet those needs and help accomplish the desired results.

- **Giving/contributing to the needs of others:** The Spirit-given ability to contribute material resources in an extraordinary way to the work of the Lord, with liberality and cheerfulness.

- **Mercy:** The Spirit-given ability to feel empathy and compassion for hurting people and then to translate that into appropriate ministry that alleviates suffering and inspires others to do the same.

- **Faith:** The Spirit-given ability to discern with extraordinary confidence the will and purpose of God and to propel the body of believers into actively believing the promises of God.

- **Healing:** The Spirit-given ability to serve as a human intermediary through whom God's healing power is applied to physical, spiritual, emotional, or other sicknesses and is evidenced when healing takes place.

- **Working of miracles:** The Spirit-given ability to serve as a human intermediary through whom it pleases God to perform powerful acts that alter or suspend the ordinary laws of nature.

- **Administration:** The Spirit-given ability to organize, direct, and implement plans to lead others in the various ministries of the church, with an emphasis on details and organization.

If you haven't considered how God has gifted you, let me encourage you to prayerfully work through this list and ask the Holy Spirit to help you recognize your gifts. Then ask someone, (a believer) who knows you well, to read through the list and give you feedback regarding what *they* see your gifts to be.

At any given time in the life of the local church or the church at work in the world, there are countless needs and places where you may be able to use your gifts in the building up of the Body of Christ.

As you serve, be always mindful that it's only by God's strength that you serve—not by your own strength or your own effort or works. It is by *his* power, for *his* purposes. Why? *"In order that in everything God may be glorified through Jesus Christ. To him belong glory and dominion forever and ever. Amen."* (1 Peter 4:11)

The end game for a church that is *captivated by the cross, motivated by love,* and *animated by grace*—a church using the serving and speaking gifts for the advancement of God's kingdom—is for God to receive glory…forever.

BETWEEN YOU AND GOD

1. When you read the way Ravi Zacharias defines radical Christianity, do you wish you could live that way or does it sound too "over the top?" Ask God to show you what radical faith would look like if practiced in your everyday world.

2. If we are to be a cross-captivated, love-motivated, and grace-animated church, which of these qualities best describe you? How are you using these qualities in service to the church?

3. Identify what you believe may be your top three or four spiritual gifts from the list provided. Think about what ministries in the church might be a good fit for those gifts and investigate how you might volunteer.

---

[1] Ravi Zacharias, *Has Christianity Failed You?* (Zondervan, 2010), 105.
[2] Zacharias, 105.
[3] Timothy Keller, September 18, 2011, Sermon Series: Every Member Ministry. Title: "Everyone with a Gift."
[4] J.I. Packer, *18 Words: The Most Important Words You Will Ever Know* (Christian Focus, 2010), 91-92.

Chapter 7

SERVE

Stewarding our Time, Talents, and Treasure

In the last chapter, Pastor Todd gave us a beautiful picture of a church that serves not out of duty, but because our hearts have been captivated by what Christ accomplished on the cross, which then motivates us to serve with love and grace. He also reminded us that God not only gave us the Holy Spirit to help us become that kind of church, but he gives every believer spiritual gifts to further equip us to serve the church and others.

Let that truth soak in. **Every believer gets gifts**. And even though spiritual gifts are not dispensed *evenly*, they are given *appropriately*. God decides because he knows us better than anyone else.

God has given you the spiritual gifts
he wants you to have,
to do the work he planned for you to do,
for the advancement of his kingdom and for his glory.

The big question, then, is this: What will you do with the gifts you've been given? It's not a rhetorical question. In 2 Corinthians 5:10 the apostle Paul writes, *"For we must all appear before the judgment seat of Christ, so that each one may receive what is due for what he has done in the body, whether good or evil."* True, we will not be judged *only* on how we've used our gifts, but it will be a component. Also, let me be clear that one's eternal destiny is not at issue in this particular judgment. This is a judgment about eternal rewards for those who are part of the Kingdom of God, based on what they have done with what they've been given.

In other words, we get spiritual gifts from God because there's work to do and we need help! And when Christ returns, each one of us will be asked to give an account to the giver of the gifts about what we've done with what we were given.

That's why **Serve** is the third of the four disciplines that make up our Rhythm of Discipleship. Serving matters. Serving is essential for the proper functioning of the church.

In most churches, 20% of the people do 80% of the work. But that's not how it's supposed to be. When 20% of the people are at the church serving all the time (because 80% aren't doing anything), collectively we will not be successful in our mission.

Remember the four components of our Rhythm of Discipleship? Worship, Grow, Serve, and Go—our shorthand job description for what it means to be a disciple of Christ? Well, your brothers and sisters in Christ may not be free to *go* with the gospel to the world and may not be free to *worship* and to *grow* with others in the Word, if everyone isn't stepping up to do their part.

Furthermore, it's not just the serving that's important. It's serving the body of Christ *with your spiritual gifts*.

Paul writes in Ephesians 4:15-16, *"Rather, speaking the truth in love, we are to grow up in every way into him who is the head, into Christ, from whom the whole body, joined and held together by every joint with which it is equipped, when each part is working properly, makes the body grow, so that it builds itself up in love."*

That last sentence is key: *"When each part is working properly."* Each part means *each one* of you. You have a role to play in the building up of the body of Christ and that's why it's so important to identify a place of service in the church where you will regularly minister to others with your time, talent, and treasure. Unless we're all using our gifts to serve the body, we can't grow to full maturity, individually or corporately.

What keeps believers from serving with their time, talents, and treasure? Here are four theories:

1. **You're not sure this church is for you**.

    You're still "kicking the tires." That's fine. But if you're still kicking the tires three years from now, you're probably in the wrong church. Let us help you find a church where you will be able to fully engage in their mission. Our goal is not for Covenant to be a big church. Our goal is to advance the Kingdom of God. If you can do that more effectively in another local community of believers, we want to help you do it!

2. **You don't know what you can do to help.**

    That's okay; we can help you get plugged in. There are activities (like our periodic Ministry Fest) and publications (like our *Covenant Monthly*) that can introduce you to multiple serving opportunities that need passionate co-laborers. You can tailor your service to the time and place and type of thing that works best for you. No arm-twisting.

    Do you like working with kids? Do you enjoy showing hospitality to visitors? Do you like organizing things? Or what about serving with the production team that handles sound, lights, and cameras? They'll train you. Or you could work with the English as a Second Language team of volunteers or pack seeds to send to poor farmers in Third

World countries. No experience required. Just a servant heart.

Have questions? A good place to start is a visit on Sunday mornings to the Welcome Desk where a volunteer can give you more specifics of how to get connected.

3. **You're afraid**.

You're afraid to step out, afraid to mess up, afraid to commit, because of what's already on your plate (which deserves its own discussion about balance and setting priorities). Or maybe you're afraid you're not a mature enough Christian. I understand. But be reassured that many serving opportunities require no extraordinary spiritual knowledge. Just a heart to love God and love others.

4. **You approach church with a lazy consumer mentality**.

Be honest. Do you have a pattern of taking without giving back? Do you find yourself going through a mental checklist, like browsing through a menu and, when the menu no longer interests you, you move to another church—taking, but never contributing? You rob the *church* that needs the time, talent, and treasure God has entrusted to you and you rob *yourself* of the spiritual benefits of using what God has given to you for kingdom purposes.

I realize it's a bit startling to see those last two issues—fear and laziness—stated so bluntly. Who wants to be called out for *that*, especially at church! Aren't we supposed to only say nice things about each other and accept where others are at on their spiritual journey?

God is our example here. He loved us enough to die for us, but he also loves us enough not to let us stay the way we are, if we're self-absorbed and living less than a gospel-transformed life.

Fear and laziness are our enemies. They keep us from being part of what God wants to do in us for his kingdom. The good news is there's a cure.

> **Knowledge of the Master frees us from fear**
> **and shakes us from laziness,**
> **so we can take risks for the Kingdom**
> **as we serve him.**

This truth is demonstrated in the parable told in Matthew 25. Let's dig deep into the story.

The Master Entrusts Resources to His Servants

Matthew 25:14 begins with a master who, *"called his servants and entrusted to them his property."* Right away, we're given important details that help us understand our own relationship to *our* Master, Jesus Christ.

The resources are his, not ours.

The servants in the parable are never called *owners* of what they possess. They are *stewards*. A steward is someone entrusted with another person's wealth or property and charged with the responsibility of managing it in the owner's best interest.

The same is true of us. We're stewards, not owners. Everything we possess belongs to the Lord. If we don't understand this, we'll constantly struggle with how to manage the time, talent, and treasure we've been given in the way God intended.

In his book *Mere Christianity,* C.S. Lewis writes, "Every faculty you have, and your power of thinking or of moving your limbs from moment to moment, is given to you by God. If you devoted every moment of your whole life exclusively to his service, you could not give him anything that was not, in a sense, his own already."[1]

Some Christians act like *they* own all that they have. They give God two or three percent of their income or other resources and see themselves as extraordinarily generous. From God's perspective, they're extraordinarily greedy—keeping 97% of *his* stuff for themselves.

God understands there's a cost of doing business in this world. There's a cost of living. Stewards have costs, fees, overhead, stuff they have to pay to manage their money and other assets. And God knows we're all in different situations, with various callings, which means those "costs" will vary from person to person. That's why God generously lets you set your own fee for managing *his* resources. But put yourself in God's shoes. How many stewards or money managers would you allow to take, as their fee, 97% of what you entrusted to them?

The correct question we should be asking ourselves is *not,* "How much of my stuff am I going to share with God to use for his purposes?" The correct question is, "How much of *God's* stuff am I going to redirect away from his purposes and keep for myself?

A good steward is careful to make sure that every decision he makes is in the best interest of the owner. Ask yourself, "Does the 'return' I'm giving God for *his* assets) justify the 'fee' I'm taking from him for what he's entrusted to me?"

This doesn't mean that you haven't studied hard, worked hard, saved, and invested wisely. Rather, it's an acknowledgment that all of it has been given to you by God and, as his servant, you've been *entrusted* to steward those resources for him.

They're Lavish Resources

The parable gets more specific in Matthew 28:15: *"To one he gave five talents, to another two, to another one."* When we hear the word "talent," we associate it with something like "America's Got Talent." But that's not how Jesus's hearers understood it.

A talent was a measure of weight. Typically, it was about 75 pounds of silver. One talent, then, would be the equivalent of about twenty years' wages for a laborer. So the master had *lavished* on these servants *enormous* resources: 100, 40, and 20 years' wages respectively.

In today's terms, a "talented" person is not one weighed down with 75 pounds of silver, but rather a person who is *gifted*. In other words, the Master has entrusted us with financial resources to steward on his behalf, but he's also given us intellectual abilities, physical abilities, artistic abilities, relational abilities and more. Like the servants in the parable, even the least talented among us is still enormously "talented." But that's not the last thing we notice.

They're Unequal Resources

The parable tells us plainly that the master distributes resources lavishly, but not equally. Matthew 28:15 says they're given *"to each according to his ability."* The proportions are different because all of us are not equally *able*. The master entrusts his lavish resources to his servants *unequally* on the basis of their abilities.

It may seem puzzling that God would choose to give some people more gifts than others, but that's the setup, even though it flies in the face of what we're often taught in our culture. Thankfully, regardless of our level of ability, God *loves* all of us equally. And our abilities—whether they are few or many—in no way affect our worth in God's eyes or the free gift of salvation he gladly offers us all.

To relate the Matthew 28 parable to our lives today, the resources we've been given by God to steward are our time, talent, and treasure.

For many of us, *time* is our most precious possession and the scarcest of our resources. But it's also the one resource we all have in equal amounts. We all get 24 hours. *Talent*, as I've said earlier, refers to our skills, gifts, abilities, and experiences. And *treasure* refers to our money, wealth, investments, and even our influence and relationships.

The Master Expects a Return On His Resources

Matthew 25:16 doesn't spell out this fact explicitly, but the passage does make clear that the first two servants understood what they were supposed to be doing while the master was away. Matthew writes about the first servant: *"He who had received the five talents went at once and traded with them, and he made five talents more."*

Furthermore, the fact that the master wanted to settle accounts immediately upon his return shows us that he expected the servants to be busy while he was gone.

When the master returns, the first servant has doubled his investment and now has ten talents. The servant who had two talents made two talents more. Another 100% return. Pretty impressive.

Unfortunately, the third servant buried his talent in the ground and simply maintained his one talent. No return on investment. We quickly learn from the master that a zero return is not acceptable.

The Expected Return Depends on the Initial Gift

The return expected by the master was in proportion to the sum entrusted. One had been entrusted with more than the other, so more was required of him, but they weren't to be compared to each other. The man who made two talents received the same commendation as the one who made five talents.

Here's what this means for you: You may be a two-talent person, a five-talent person, or a one-talent person. If you're a one-talent person, you don't have to worry that God expects you to come up with the same return as a five-talent person. God recognizes each of us as different. He only expects of us what is appropriate in light of what we've been given.

One of the temptations for the one-talent and two-talent people is to look at five-talent people and say, "Well I can never give as much as them, or serve as well as them, so why even try." You get discouraged because you think the master is going to evaluate your returns on the basis of *their* talents and returns, not *yours*. It's not true.

On the flip side, the temptation is for five-talent servants to look at one-talent and two-talent servants' "returns" and feel satisfied with how much more they've done for the kingdom than those given lesser talents. They would be wrong. You're not more loved by God or more special or more valuable to the church just because you've been entrusted with more.

**You won't be judged
for what you've done in comparison to *others*.
You'll be judged for what you've done
with what the master gave *you*.**

In the parable, the one-talent servant was not judged for failing to gain the same returns as those with more talents. He was judged for failing to use what he had.

This leads us to another important truth:

Producing Returns for the Master Requires Risk

Everyone involved in any kind of business enterprise understands that rewards require risk-taking. This isn't only true in business; it's true in relationships. If you're single and you'd like to be married, you're going to have to take a risk and accept a date or ask her to marry you. In our relationship with Jesus, if we're going to follow him, it requires that we take the risk of faith and obey his commands, even when we can't see how it will work out.

The first two servants take what's been entrusted to them and venture out into the world, taking risks with their talents, to advance their master's interests. The third servant is the definition of risk-averse. He refuses to take a risk with what's been entrusted to him, choosing rather to bury it in the ground. The third servant opts for safety instead of service. **"Hoping to avoid doing anything wrong, he finished up by not doing anything right."[2]** [Emphasis added.]

Does that sound like you? Personally, I don't like to make mistakes. I don't like things that are messy. I like to think things through, I like to have a plan, and I like to know how things are going to play out. That's a strength in some areas of my life, but God has convicted me in a big way that it's definitely wrong in other areas.

For example, I love Jesus and I know that apart from him my friends and family members will not go to heaven. I believe it with all my heart. I know I should share the gospel with them, and I *want* to share the gospel with them. But I'm afraid. I don't know how it will go. It could get messy. I might make a mistake. So what do I do? Nothing. I bury the opportunities God has given me, thinking it's better to do nothing than to mess up. *And I couldn't be more wrong.* I've told God I'm sorry for that attitude and have asked him to help me do better, with the Holy Spirit's help.

Risk is at the heart of discipleship.

You can't follow Jesus without risk! I'm committing to taking a risk in some of my relationships, trusting that obedience and seeking a return for my master is far better than trying not to mess up. When you really think about it biblically, what's the greater risk? Attempting something for God's kingdom and failing? Or burying your talent and not using what the master has entrusted to you? This parable teaches us the latter choice is far worse.

Several months ago I spent about nine days in India and Nepal with the leaders of Big Life, a disciple-making ministry that our church supports. John Heerema founded Big Life a number of years ago when he was the happy owner of a business, making good money, playing lots of golf, and not having a care in the world.

But God started working on him. John grew concerned that maybe he was succeeding at something that didn't matter. He and his wife felt God was leading them to sell the business and use the proceeds to start Big Life. They had no idea what they were doing. The risk was enormous. But John shared with me what tipped the scales for them.

"I imagined myself standing before God on the last day," he said. "I decided I would rather fail at Big Life and say, 'God I thought it was what you wanted me to do,' than to keep the business and say, 'I was afraid to take a risk.'"

That's biblical thinking. And that risk has been a catalyst for the transformation of over 200,000 lives and counting.

Likewise, Bob Petterson, my predecessor and mentor at Covenant Church, had a great job here for fourteen years as Senior Pastor. He had a good income, he had strong support from the leadership and the church body, and he enjoyed the ministry.

He could have coasted in that role to the finish line. But he and his wife Joyce felt God calling them to step out in faith and take a risk to pursue a speaking and writing ministry that has the potential to impact many more lives than they could have done had they played it safe.

Listen, nothing in this parable says we're to be foolish and not make plans and not think things through. No! We're to use God's gifts responsibly, but we're to *use* them. Adventurously!

You and I have permission to do what British missionary and social reformer William Carey said: "Expect great things from God. Attempt great things for God." Carey is often called the Father of Modern Missions. He translated the entire Bible into six languages and portions of the Bible into 29 other languages, although he never attended the equivalent of high school or college. He did, indeed, attempt great things for God and he achieved them.[3]

Notice one other thing in this parable:

There is *no* example of a servant
who took a risk and had *no* return on investment.
The only one who has *no* return
is the one who *refused* to take a risk.

Ultimately, if God's glory is our desire and his kingdom is our goal, the only way to fail is not to try. Why not step out and take a risk?

The third servant plainly reveals that fear was at the root of his disobedience. Matthew 25:24 says, *"Master, I knew you to be a hard man, reaping where you did not sow, and gathering where you scattered no seed, so I was afraid."* He clearly understands his master desires profit. Yet his fear of messing up, of taking a risk, lands him in a place of disobedience and, ultimately, condemnation.

The master says later in verse 27, *"Then you ought to have invested my money with the bankers, and at my coming, I should have received what was my own with interest."* In other words, the master would've accepted even the tiniest risk of putting the money in the bank, so at least there would be interest. But even that was too scary for the play-it-safe servant.

God hasn't put us here on this earth to play it safe. He's put us here to advance the kingdom and make disciples.

Risk-taking required.

We need the mentality of William Carey, who packed all his belongings in a casket when he went to India as a missionary because he expected to die there: "I'm not afraid of failure," Carey said. "I'm afraid of being successful at things that don't matter." God, give us hearts like William Carey's.

*   *   *

And so we return to our original question: What are you doing with what's been entrusted to you? Some of us have enormous amounts of God's resources saved up and put away safely in the ground, like the servant in the parable. That's not bad by itself. Just don't forget that the master is coming and he expects to see a return on what he entrusted to you.

If all we've got to show for our lives is that we kept ourselves financially secure until we died, we're going to be more than a little ashamed when we stand before Jesus and he asks for a rundown on what we've done with what he gave us.

What are you willing to risk for his kingdom? You may not be financially secure, so sitting on your money is not your issue. But you may have exceptional gifts for helping people through mercy ministries, for example—gifts that you're not using. For others, it may be musical gifts or leadership gifts. When are you going to start using what he's given to you?

Some of you have been entrusted with enormous influence accumulated over a lifetime of achievements. What are you going to do with it? Let's get busy leveraging what we have for the kingdom of God, so we won't get caught holding a bunch of unused talents when he returns.

The Master Will Return to Settle Accounts

The parable concludes with the master returning to settle accounts. The Bible tells us that Jesus, too, is coming again. On that day, two things will happen. The parable gives us a preview:

The Faithful Will Be Rewarded

The two successful servants receive identical commendations even though their level of responsibility was different. The master says in Matthew 24:21, *"Well done, good and faithful servant. You have been faithful over a little; I will set you over much. Enter into the joy of your master."*

Notice the reward. It's not release from slavery or responsibility. Rather, the reward for faithful stewardship is to be entrusted with more responsibility! Where is this added responsibility given? Here on earth? Well, certainly those on earth who are faithful with what God has given are rewarded with more. But the focus in this passage of Scripture is about life in the new heavens and the new earth when Christ returns.

Many Christians mistakenly think that the goal of life is simply to get into heaven and to do the least amount possible to get there. The truth is this: None of us gets to heaven by what we've done—whether little or much. The only way to get to heaven is by trusting in Jesus Christ who did it all *for* us by his death on the cross.

However—after the resurrection and the restoration of all things—while *everyone's* enjoyment will be full, it will not be equal. The lifelong rebel who makes a deathbed confession will not share the same reward as the faithful believer who walked with Christ for 65 years. Neither of them will be dissatisfied with their eternal inheritance in any way. The joy of both will be full in heaven, but the capacity for joy will vary.

For example, John Piper suggests that our generosity here on earth builds the size of the cup God will use in giving back to us in heaven. All of our cups will overflow, but some of us will have larger cups than others.[4]

The Bible very clearly teaches that there are rewards for the faithful in heaven that the less faithful will not experience. Some will have greater responsibility and thus greater joy in heaven than others, because of how they've faithfully stewarded what God has entrusted to them on earth. Jesus is clear: We should be diligent to store up treasures in heaven so that, Scripture implies, we will be able to enjoy them with him there. (See Luke 19:17-19, 2 Cor. 3:12-15, 2 Cor. 5:9-10.)

We've largely lost sight of this New Testament teaching. Consequently, it doesn't motivate us to live the life of faith to the hilt as Jesus intended. May this truth re-energize us to serve God with all our hearts.

The faithful will be rewarded in heaven according to what they've done with what they had on earth.

A word of clarification is appropriate. Our good deeds here on earth do not win our *salvation*. **Salvation and rewards are not the same things.** Salvation is a free gift, which is only received through faith in Christ. It cannot be earned or deserved or worked for. Salvation is for those who have asked God to forgive their sins and have entered into a personal relationship with Christ. At the judgment that is described in 2 Corinthians 5:10, God then gives rewards to his people in response to how we have lived the Christian life after we made our profession of faith here on earth.

The Fearful Will Be Judged

In the parable, after the master rewards the two faithful servants, he addresses the fearful servant. *"You wicked and slothful servant!"* (Matthew 24:26) Tough language. Why was this servant wicked and slothful? Could it be because he didn't really know his master?

Matthew Henry, a 17th Puritan preacher, writes, "This ill affection toward God arose from his false notions of him, and nothing is more unworthy of God, nor more hinders our duty to him, than slavish fear."

The fearful servant understood God to be a slavish taskmaster, demanding his pound of flesh. He did not fully grasp nor receive the gospel. Ultimately, this servant is not condemned so much because he didn't give the master a return, but rather because he didn't know and love the master himself.

So what kind of master do we have? Is he a slave-master who abuses his servants and gives nothing in return? Or is he the wealthy God who not only has given us gifts of time, talent, and treasure, but the gift of his one and only Son? Do you realize what God has given you by giving you Jesus?

- You have the forgiveness of sin.
- You have eternal life.
- You have the Holy Spirit working transformation in your life.
- You have the assurance of God's love and constant care.

- You have every spiritual blessing in the heavenly places.
- You have the promise of the resurrection and an eternity of reigning with Christ in the new heavens and new earth.
- You have eternal rewards awaiting you that correspond to how you used what God entrusted to you on this earth.

You have nothing to fear.

If we mistakenly view God as a hard taskmaster, it will be hard to respond to him in a loving and open way. But we have a Father who loves us and it brings him *great joy* to see us take kingdom risks in his name. It brings him *great joy* to reward us for doing so.

Martin Luther used to say, "There are only two days on my calendar: today and *that* Day." Are you living for *that* day or for today? May we serve the Lord with our time, talents, and treasure, in light of *that day*.

Think what could happen if our mission—to develop and deploy fully devoted followers of Jesus Christ to disciple our family, community, and world—was carried out by bold, risk-taking, servant-hearted believers, who *know* their master and fear nothing but squandering what he has generously given.

100

BETWEEN YOU AND GOD

1. Does it feel too radical to view your time, talent and treasure as *all* belonging to God, with you acting as a steward and not an owner? Talk to God about it. Be specific about what's hardest and ask his help in realigning your view of this to God's point of view.

2. What do your checkbook and personal calendar tell you about what are your priorities? What needs adjusting?

3. Name one step you're willing to take to serve in a way you've never done or have not done recently. Tell a Christian friend about it and ask them to hold you accountable to act.

[1] C. S. Lewis, "Faith," *Mere Christianity,* (New York, MacMillan Publishing Co., 21st Ed., 1975), 110.
[2] R.T. France, *The Gospel of Matthew, New Bible Commentary 21st Century Edition* (IVP Academic, 2010), *938.*
3 R.E. Hedland, "Wm. Carey: Did You Know?" *Christian History Magazine, Issue 36, Christianity Today,* http://www.christianitytoday.com/history/issues/issue-36/william-carey-did-you-know.html *(1992).*
[4] John Piper, http://www.desiringgod.org/interviews/will-some-people-in-heaven-have-more-joy-than-others.

Chapter 8

GO

Proclaim Good News

"Preach the gospel at all times. Use words if necessary." You've probably heard that quote before, particularly if you've been around the world of Christianity for any amount of time. It's typically attributed to the 13th-century Catholic monk Saint Francis of Assisi. The quote reminds us that our lives should be the clearest evidence of our message. There's truth to that. But the quote is also misleading because it misunderstands the nature of the gospel.

Tim Keller writes, "If the gospel were primarily about *what we must do* to be saved, it could be communicated as well by actions (to be imitated) as by words. But, if the gospel is primarily about *what God has done* to save us and how we can receive it through faith, it can only be expressed through words. Faith cannot come without hearing."[1]

In other words, although our good example can attract people toward faith, it isn't enough. If people say, "I want to be like that person," they still need to hear what happened to that person that made them who they are. They need to hear the story spoken of how Christ's death and resurrection paid their sin debt, transformed them from the inside out, and secured eternity for them. Then those hearers must *accept* and *act* on the truth of those words.

If we look more closely at the life of St. Francis, it's clear that, despite his famous quote, apparently, he, too, understood the importance of proclaiming God's good news, because, it turns out, he was quite the preacher.

Mark Galli in *Christianity Today* writes that Francis sometimes preached in up to five villages a day, often outdoors.

> In the country, Francis often spoke from a bale of straw or a granary doorway. In town, he would climb on a box or up steps in a public building. He preached to serfs and their families as well as to the landholders, to merchants, women, clerks, and priests—any who gathered to hear the strange but fiery little preacher from Assisi.[2]

Why was Francis such a prodigious proclaimer of the gospel *through words*? Because, as we've said, unless someone *proclaims* the gospel, those without faith cannot be saved. The Apostle Paul makes the same point in Romans 10:14: *"How then will they call on him in whom they have not believed? And how are they to believe in him of whom they have never heard? And how are they to hear without someone preaching?"*

**We must GO, *proclaim* the gospel,
and send others to do the same.**

This command is so exquisitely simple, it doesn't take a long defense. But there are two key takeaways I want you to consider:

- There's a *promise* connected to the gospel that should motivate every believer to share the good news.

- There's a *need* that makes clear why words are required.

The PROMISE that Motivates Missions

If you look at the context of Romans 10, you'll see that until now the Apostle Paul has been explaining why the Jews of his day were missing out on salvation, while the Gentiles were receiving it. This was puzzling for one main reason: The gospel boldly offers its promise to all people without distinction. That's the promise in Romans 10:13, *"For everyone who calls on the name of the Lord will be saved."*

Let's break down that promise:

"Everyone"

When Paul says "everyone" he's making a universal offer of the gospel to all people, without exceptions. The gospel came first to the Jews, but it was never intended to stop there. When God called Abraham in Genesis 12:1-3, he explained his intention was to bless all the nations of the earth through Abraham, not just to bless the Jews. In fact, it was not just an intention. It was a promise.

This is precisely what we happens in Revelation 7:9-10 when John writes, *"After this I looked, and behold, a great multitude that no one could number, from every nation, from all tribes and peoples and languages, standing before the throne and before the Lamb, clothed in white robes, with palm branches in their hands, and crying out with a loud voice, 'Salvation belongs to our God who sits on the throne, and to the Lamb!'"*

What an amazing picture. Think about it. All of history is moving toward this incredible moment. Chinese, Bolivians, Saudis, Afghanis, Navajos, Ethiopians, Democrats, Libertarians, Republicans, rednecks, Rothschilds, and more have this promise held out to them.

"Who calls on the name of the Lord"

While the promise is held out to everyone, it is still necessary for people to *respond* to the good news of the gospel and call upon the Lord. To call on the name of the Lord is to appeal to him to save us, according to who he is and what he's done for us.

In fact, anyone reading these words who has never made a conscious decision to respond to the gospel can stop right now and call out to God in the quietness of your heart. All it takes is a simple, heartfelt prayer. There are no "perfect" words to say. You can express your desire in your own words, but it might sound something like this: "Lord Jesus, have mercy on me! I believe you died on the cross for my sins and that you rose again, ensuring that I will spend eternity with you. Thank you from the bottom of my heart. I want to be a different person. My desire is to be free from the guilt and condemnation of sin and to live my life now for you."

For those who call out to God in this way, he makes a take-it-to-the-bank promise:

[You] "Will be saved"

You will be saved! Saved from what? Saved from slavery to sin and the misery it creates in our lives. Saved from death, which is the consequence we deserve for sin. Saved from the wrath of God that's coming on the whole world, because of the world's rejection of God and his truth. Once you accept Christ as your personal Savior, your debt is paid! Welcome to the family of God. *"Everyone who calls on the name of the Lord will be saved."* (Rom. 10:13)

What, then, do saved people do? With joy and gratitude, they choose to live a new way. They grow and commit themselves to becoming fully devoted followers of Christ. They practice spiritual disciplines that help them grow. As you've heard throughout this book, it's what we call a natural Rhythm of Discipleship—Worship, Grow, Serve, and Go. They glorify God and want to obey him because they love him.

For those of us already part of God's family, it's a big deal to see this human transformation take place. New life. Hope. Purpose. That's why we long to see more and more people love, worship, and glorify God.

Admittedly, not all people see themselves in a state of misery apart from God. Their hearts may not yet have been overwhelmed by God's love and the great gift he offers. We were all in their place at some point. Our role is to love them. Pray for them. Give them space. The last chapter of their story has not yet been written and God is patient.

However, many others are desperate and *do* recognize their condition. They long to hear that there's a different way to live and they're ready to consider God now. They need to hear it from us. They need to hear that extraordinary promise:

All people everywhere--no matter who they are,
what they've done, what they've believed,
who they've worshiped--
everyone
who calls on the name of the Lord
will be saved.

The NEED that Requires Missions

Right after Paul gives us this amazing promise about salvation in Romans 10:14, he makes a strong case for missions by asking four key questions:

Question 1: *"How, then, will they call on him in whom they have not believed?"*

Paul's Point: People can't call on Jesus if they don't *believe* in him.

> The only way people will call upon the Lord to save them is if they believe they *need* saving and they believe Jesus is the one who can save them.

Question 2: *"And how are they to believe in him of whom they have never heard?"*

Paul's Point: People can't believe in Jesus if they haven't *heard* of him.

> The Bible is clear: there is salvation from sin and the coming wrath of God only through trusting in Jesus. There is no other way to the Father, except the salvation offered through Jesus. What if no one tells them?

Question 3: *"And how are they to hear without someone preaching?"*

Paul's Point: People can't hear of Jesus if someone doesn't *proclaim* him.

> I suspect most of you reading this who are believers became Christians because someone at some point told you about Jesus. There are occasionally people who come to faith because they have encountered Jesus through a dream. (This is happening with a surprising amount of frequency in the Muslim world.) Additionally, there are some people who hear of Jesus because they discover a Bible in a hospital or hotel room, placed there by the Gideons, and they simply start reading it and God speaks to them through

his Word. But most of the time people hear about Jesus because someone personally *proclaimed* him.

As hard as it may seem to those of us in the western world, there are many people in the world who do not know a single Christian who might proclaim Jesus to them. It's hard to nail down an exact number, but one estimate is that there are nearly two billion people who live on the same planet as us, who have not heard of Jesus—at least not in such a way that they would know and understand how to put their trust in him for salvation.[3] That leads us to Paul's fourth question in Romans 10:15.

Question 4: *"And how are they to preach unless they are sent?"*

Paul's Point: People can't preach to unreached people about Jesus if they aren't sent.

Paul probably had two things in mind when he used the word "sent." First, Christ sent us authoritative witnesses and proclaimers when he sent the apostles, whose message is contained in the Bible.

But, secondly, today Christ, through the local church, also sends out missionaries, preachers, and fully devoted followers of Christ in all places and at all times to be messengers of that same good news.

In one way or another, we're *all* sent. He may send us into a pulpit, overseas, or simply across the street to talk to our neighbor. But ours are to be "the beautiful feet bringing good news," that Paul talks about in Romans 10:15.

Again, it's exquisitely simple:

The promise that motivates us to engage in proclaiming the gospel is that everyone who believes the message we proclaim and who calls upon the Lord will be saved.

But the gospel needs proclaimers. Unless the gospel is proclaimed, sinners will not hear how they may be saved, they will not believe in Christ's life, death, and resurrection, and they will not call on him. And unless they call on him, they will not be saved.

We, of course, can't save anyone or make anyone believe. It's all God's doing. But, as Tim Keller writes, we have an important role to play: "We must ensure that, wherever it is that God has placed us, no one around us can say they have not heard or understood."[4]

Does the task seem daunting? Where do we start? Here are a few simple tips:

The Response that Accelerates Missions

Confirm Your Own Salvation

If you have not trusted Christ personally to take away your sin, don't delay. There's only one way to be on God's "good side." It's to place your trust in his Son, Jesus, who died so you could live now with peace and purpose in this world until you die and then live forever with him for all eternity.

Go and Proclaim Good News to Others

If you've believed the good news about what Jesus has done for you, share it. Look for people who are receptive to the message and ready to talk about it. Share in a way that is respectful, gentle, and kind. Don't get preoccupied with how good or bad a person looks on the outside. Let God worry about that. He is able and willing to provide salvation to all who believe. That's all that matters.

You may not lead a person all the way across the threshold to faith; you may just lead them to the next step. But look around you at your family, community, and your larger world and be alert to opportunities to share the good news every week.

And, remember, once you've personally committed your life to Christ, you have your own story of faith to share, too. A personal testimony is a powerful thing. No one can refute it. It's *your* story and it's true. Share it. It's all part of our individual and collective mandate to *go* and share the gospel.

The late Harvie Conn, an expert on missions and methods for sharing the gospel, pointed out that, "One cannot be a missionary church and continue insisting that the world must come to the church on the church's terms. It must become a 'go' structure. And it can do that only when its concerns are directed outside itself toward the poor, the abused, and the oppressed."

**The church must recapture its identity as
the only organization in the world
that exists for the sake of its non-members.**[5]

Covenant is a missions church. God called us out from the bad news all around us in the world and brought us the good news of the gospel. But he didn't do it so we could hunker down in a holy huddle until he returns. Rather, he says, "Take my good news and spread it around. Saturate all that bad news with *better* news. Tell them my story." Every believer has been commissioned by Jesus to *go*.

Where You Can't Go, Pray for More Workers

In John 4:35, Scripture uses the metaphor that the fields (people everywhere) are "white for harvest" (ready to hear). That means people are waiting, but more proclaimers are needed!

Most of us will simply stay in our homes and make disciples as we go about our daily lives. That's a God-given mission and not to be disparaged as, somehow, a lesser calling. But we should also be praying that Jesus would call some to "go" farther—to another community, another people group, or even another nation. And, as you pray for more workers, be sensitive to the fact that Jesus might even be asking you to consider a foreign assignment, to go *beyond* your community to the world.

Where You Can't Go, Leverage Resources to Send Others

That's what our global missions program is all about. Most of us don't have the ability to reach people in the villages of India. We can't proclaim the good news to them, but others can if they are funded. So we can give money, for example, to support scooter teams that will proclaim the gospel to people we can't personally speak to in the farthest corners of India. You probably aren't able to proclaim the gospel to the people in the Parramore Avenue area in Orlando, but you can support a church planter who is doing so.

You may have a lot of money to send others or just a little. That's not the point. The point is this: what are you doing with what you've got?

Each year everyone who calls our church home has the opportunity to make what we call a Faith Promise Pledge. It's when we have the opportunity to pray about giving through our missions fund to one or several missions organizations at home and abroad, that have all been vetted for their legitimacy and effectiveness. It's a time to huddle with our families and talk about how we personally want to advance God's kingdom purposes in the world. We invite our Covenant family to get creative and even consider taking a little risk in how we're giving, to help make sure the whole world hears the Good News about Jesus.

The *Go* piece of our Rhythm of Discipleship requires no exhaustive theological training. It requires an awareness of what God expects of us and a willingness to act.

God made it clear that everyone who calls upon the name of the Lord will be saved. But he also made clear that *only* those who call on the name of the Lord will be saved, so more proclaimers are needed. You, me, or others whom we may help to send with our resources. It's all part of our oft-repeated Mission Statement:

To develop and deploy
fully devoted followers of Christ,
to disciple our family, community, and world.

BETWEEN YOU AND GOD

1. What part of sharing the gospel feels the easiest and what feels like the hardest part? Pray through with God whether you have made the hard parts an excuse for not being bolder.

2. What is a concrete first step you could take to become more *Go*-oriented?

3. Name three people in your circles of influence who do not have a personal relationship with Christ. Set aside their objections to faith or your belief that they are unlikely to be open to God. Just pray that the Holy Spirit would create a natural way for you to talk with them about God.

---

[1] Tim Keller, *Center Church: Doing Balanced, Gospel-Centered Ministry in Your City* (Zondervan, 2012), 32.

[2] Mark Galli, "Speak the Gospel: Use Deeds When Necessary," *Christianity Today*, May 21, 2009.

[3] *https://joshuaproject.net/resources/articles/has_everyone_heard*.

[4] Keller, *Center Church, Doing Balanced, Gospel-Centered Ministry in Your City*, 84.

[5] Quoted in the book by C. John Miller, *Powerful Evangelism for the Powerless*, 22 (P & R Publishing, 1997).

Chapter 9

GO

Do Good Works

Few people want to be called zealous these days. A zealous person is sometimes seen as unthinking, intolerant, and maybe even violent. Those may be fitting descriptors of some zealous people, but zeal can be a wonderful thing if appropriately exercised.

Bill Gates would be the first person to admit he was zealous about software. In fact, he credits his obsession with helping him rise to the top. On his blog, he wrote, "When I was in my 20s and early 30s, I was fanatical about software. By 'fanatical' I mean that I was so focused on my vision of putting a computer on every desk and in every home that I gave up a normal existence."

Getting into work early, staying late, and working hard, impressed his colleagues. While many people his age were thinking about marriage or travel, he focused on innovating. Who could argue with what Gates achieved through his zeal and his vision of a personal computer for everyone? But, as he said, his zeal for this one thing led him to give up a normal existence.

If you look at people who have risen to the top of nearly any field—whether it is science, medicine, business, the arts, or athletics—every one of them would be marked by zeal, an unswerving dedication to a goal. As the late British politician Charles Buxton said, "Experience shows that success is due less to ability than to zeal."

In Titus 2:11-14, the apostle Paul reminds us that when Jesus went to the cross, his intention was to ignite the hearts of people so they would be zealous to do good works. *Passionate* for good works. People who get up in the morning eager to do good and who go to bed at night thinking about how they can do good tomorrow. It's the kind of life that should mark us as Christians. It's one of the primary ways we can proclaim the Good News to the world. In Matthew 5:16, Jesus said, *"Let your light so shine before others, so that they may see your good works and give glory to your Father who is in heaven."*

What if we were so zealous about doing good works in the world that—like Bill Gates—we were actually willing to give up a normal existence? Imagine the impact we could have in our community. Imagine the impact we could have on the world!

What will *motivate* us to do these zealous good works? What will *equip* us to do them? What will *sustain* us when we're trying to do good but not seeing the fruits of our labor? What will *inspire* us to actually alter our lives to be a blessing to others?

Is it guilt? Is it feeling pressured by the biblical commands? No. It's the grace, hope, and love offered by the gospel. It's the power of God planted in us that makes us zealous for good works.

This touches on an issue where Christians sometimes get confused. Some Christians believe that when you die and stand before God, he is either going to accept you or reject you based on the quantity or quality of your good works. That's just not true.

As I mentioned in the last chapter, from this moment on, if you did good deeds *all* the time *every* moment for the rest of your life, you would not be good enough to be accepted by God.

God doesn't save good people.
He saves sinners.
Good works don't save people.
Saved people do good works.

Some of you *think* you believe that "Jesus accepts me; therefore, I want to do good out of gratitude and devotion." But your heart and life seem to operate from an opposite point of view that says, "If I do enough good things for the kingdom, Jesus will love and accept me." That is not a gospel-centered understanding of good works.

If you live with the latter mindset, when you're diligent to do good works you'll be proud and look down on people who don't do as many good works as you. Or, alternatively, if you don't feel like you're living up to the standard, you'll be depressed and condemn yourself all the time for not doing more.

Instead of being motivated by pride or guilt to do good works, Christ offers grace, hope, and love to motivate us. Let's talk about how that works.

Grace *Trains* Us for Good Works

Paul tells us in Titus 2:11: *"The grace of God has appeared."* What's he referring to? He's referring to Christ showing up on planet Earth—his life, his death for sinners, and his resurrection. In other words, God sent his Son and called him the very personification of grace. Christ was grace with skin on, *"bringing salvation for all people."*

Does that mean *everyone* automatically gets salvation? No. As we've talked about earlier, only those who have trusted in Christ will be saved. So what does Paul mean? He does not mean all people *without exception.* He means all people, *without distinction,* whether Jew or Gentile, slave or free, from every tribe, people, and nation. Grace in the flesh, Jesus, has come to offer salvation, but people still must be told the good news and actually receive it.

Grace Trains Us to Say No

The grace of God does more than just appear in the form of Christ to bring us salvation. Titus 2:12 says grace is also *"training us to renounce ungodliness and worldly passions."* This is such beautiful word picture. It shows clearly that we don't receive grace *because* we've renounced ungodliness and worldly passions. Rather, the order is this: we received the unmerited favor of God (grace) and the *effect* is that this grace trains us to say no to ungodliness and worldly passions.

Why are we now able to say no to things that are ungodly (unlike God)? Why can we now say no to our worldly passions like greed, lust, and power? Because we've tasted something better.

Sin promises satisfaction. It says, "Engage your lust and you'll be satisfied! Buy that new toy and it will scratch that itch, that discontent! Spread that bad report you heard about another person and you'll feel superior! Keep experimenting, pushing limits, and you'll find what you're looking for and what your heart desires." That kind of satisfaction, however, is short-lived.

> **Grace trains us to say no to those things,**
> **because we realize the love we long for**
> **and the significance we crave**
> **are found in Jesus.**

The more we understand the benefits of the grace we've been given, the more we're able to say no to less satisfying alternatives.

This isn't just something that unbelieving people have to learn. People who believe in Christ have to be trained by grace, too. As a Christian, you may find satisfaction and take pride in your good reputation, your generous giving, your disciplined Bible study practices, your active prayer life, or your good works in the community. Do those things make you feel valued, accepted, and loved by God? Do you realize that's the same kind of ungodliness found in the unbelievers? It's simply sin in religious garb.

Grace trains us to say no to any notion that our relationship with God has anything to do with what *we've* done. Grace reminds us that our salvation and worth are all *God's* doing. *His* initiative. *His* gift.

Grace Trains Us to Say Yes

In addition to God's grace, *"training us to renounce ungodliness and worldly passions,"* Titus 2:12 says grace also trains us to say yes to living *"self-controlled, upright, and godly lives in the present age."* These three words (self-controlled, upright, godly) perfectly describe a life of grace, because grace (or the lack of it) can affect our relationship with ourselves, with others, and our relationship to God.

Self-control is grace applied to ourselves. We choose not to do whatever we feel like doing or to say what we feel like saying because we no longer live considering only what *we* want or how *we* feel. Grace has freed us from selfishness and self-centeredness. Now we consider our actions in accordance with how it impacts God and others.

Upright refers to acting justly and righteously (moral, virtuous, irreproachable) toward other people. Grace trains us to treat other people well, even those who mistreat us, because we're aware of the grace God has extended to us, even though we, too, are undeserving. (Ps. 103:10 in the NIV says, *"He does not treat us as our sins deserve."*)

Godliness speaks to a burning desire to honor God in every word, thought, and action, whether with others or in private.

Grace makes us want to be like Christ, the One who has loved us so well.

So Christ calls us to avoid the ditch on both sides of the road. On one side, Christian spirituality is not simply saying no to certain sinful practices. People who live with a *no* mentality are inclined toward legalism, hard-heartedness, and self-righteousness because they see godliness primarily in terms of what you *don't* do.

On the other hand, other believers are so focused on saying *yes* to things like love and compassion, they don't pay attention to the clear don'ts spelled out in God's Word. Consequently, their attitudes and actions can be morally ambiguous or careless.[1]

Grace doesn't train us to say yes *or* no.
It trains us to say yes *and* no.

When we are trained by grace in this way, when the gospel sinks down deep into every part of our hearts and minds, then we're ready to do works that are truly good.

We don't have to wait until we get to heaven for this transformation to happen. The Bible is clear: this training is happening in us now, allowing us to live self-controlled, upright, and godly lives *"in the present age."*

The more deeply we're trained by grace how to live and act in the world and the more we understand that our standing with God is not based on our good works, the more we'll find ourselves eager to do truly good works and to do them with zeal.

Hope *Sustains* Us In Good Works

As you begin to intentionally "do good" in the world, you'll find that there's a whole lot of brokenness around you. You'll find people who resist the good you're trying to do. You might work hard at something for a long time, with not much to show for it. That's why it's important to understand two important things about the hope that will keep you going as you seek to "do good."

The Hope in Jesus' Return

While grace trains us to live a godly life *now,* Titus 2:13 reminds us the best is yet to come. We are *"waiting for our blessed hope, the appearing of the glory of our great God and Savior Jesus Christ."*

Scripture here speaks of Christ's "appearing" rather than his "coming." Why is that? As we look around the world, we do not see the world under the authority of Christ. Even though he is alive and well and reigning in heaven, he is, nevertheless, unseen. But one day, that hidden glory will be revealed for all to see. As one writer says, "When Christ comes, we will not see anything that is *new.* What is different is that we will *see* it."[2]

> **This *hope* is a gift that can sustain us**
> **when we can't see that our "doing good"**
> **is doing any good!**

Christ is coming back! He will appear and everyone will finally see and acknowledge him. When that day comes, a second reason to hope will also emerge: a complete overhaul of the way things are.

The Hope of Jesus's Restoration of All Things

Whether you are a follower of Christ or not, nearly all of us would agree that this world, as we see it, is not the way it's supposed to be.

Christians believe that the problem with the world began with the introduction of sin and human rebellion against God. Sin alienated us from our Creator. The solution to the sin problem, ultimately, was the death of Christ, who paid the sin debt we owed to God. Christ made a way for us to be reconciled to God and become part of God's magnificent restoration project.

He will make all things new. He will come in great glory, to judge the world and put an end to all evil, suffering, and death. What great news! Do you feel hope rising?

This picture of Christ's return and the restoration of all things should not prompt us to hide out in a holy huddle until he returns. Rather, we should revel in our standing with Christ.

- He has *already* delivered us from the *penalty* of sin.

- He is *currently* delivering us from the *power* of sin.

- He will *one day* deliver us permanently from the very *presence* of sin.

That means we can joyfully give ourselves to good works, knowing that our work will not be in vain. New Testament scholar N.T. Wright explains it in practical terms:

> What you do in the present—by painting, preaching, singing, sewing, praying, teaching, building hospitals, digging wells, campaigning for justice, writing poems, caring for the needy, loving your neighbor as yourself—will last into God's future. These activities are not simply ways of making the present life a little less beastly, a little more bearable, until the day when we leave it behind altogether. ... They are part of what we may call building for God's kingdom.[3]

It is that hope of Jesus' return and restoration of all things that sustains us in our commitment to do good works. *"And let us not grow weary of doing good, for in due season we will reap, if we do not give up."* (Galatians 6:9)

So we've seen *the grace that trains us* for good works and *the hope that sustains us* in good works. Let's take a look at the third motivator, *the love that inspires* us to good works.

Love *Inspires* Us to Good Works

Titus 2:14 speaks of Jesus, *"who gave himself for us to redeem us from all lawlessness and to purify for himself a people for his own possession who are zealous for good works."*

There's that word again: zealous. God's Word shows *love*—four kinds of love—can inspire us to zealously do good works.

Sacrificial Love

The text says he *gave* himself for us. That's sacrifice. When we recognize and reflect on the amazing fact that Christ gave himself for us, we will be inspired to give ourselves for others in his name. "Amazing love, how can it be, that Thou my God should die for me?" Who else has loved you like that?

Liberating Love

Christ gave himself to redeem us and set us free. Set us free from what? Lawlessness. Isn't that something? You may think that rules and laws constrain you and that being *without* laws (being lawless) would be liberating. But just the opposite is true. The reality is that lawlessness is the true slavery. To not know

God's heart, to not know why you were made or how to live in this world is a type of terrifying bondage. With no moral compass or loving Heavenly Father to guide you, your life is dependent on your own wisdom. Does that make you feel safe and secure?

In Romans 6:17-18 Paul says, *"But thanks be to God, that you who were once slaves of sin have become obedient from the heart to the standard of teaching to which you were committed, and, having been set free from sin, have become slaves of righteousness."* Paul says we're all slaves to something. Why not be a slave to Christ and his love and goodness?

Purifying Love

The problem with lawlessness is not only that it enslaves us, but it also defiles us. Sin carries with it a genuine moral guilt like a stain that we cannot remove. Not only does that sin defile us, but it also prevents us from having fellowship with the God who is perfect and without sin. In this passage, the apostle Paul is teaching us that when Christ died on the cross he not only liberated us from our slavery to sin, but he also cleansed us from the guilt of sin. The love of Christ on the cross served to purify us from the guilt and pollution of sin, so that we can once again have a relationship with God.

Compelling Love

When you add up the sacrificial, liberating, purifying love of Christ, does it not *compel* us toward good works? *"For the love of Christ controls us, because we have concluded this: that one has died for all, therefore all have died; and he died for all, that those who live might no longer live for themselves but for him who for their sake died and was raised."* (2 Corinthians 5:14-15)

We've been set free by Christ to be generous, helpful, and to contribute positively to others and the world around us. He is creating a people who are part of the new creation God is making of this world. What a privilege to join him in this great adventure.

Grace trains us,
Hope sustains us,
Love inspires us,
to proclaim the good news
while doing good works.

Do you see more clearly now how our Rhythm of Discipleship —Worship, Grow, Serve and Go—represents the full circle of the life of faith?

- **When we worship**, we focus on the greatness and goodness of God and we hear the Good News of the gospel through the preaching of the Word.

- **When we grow**, we spend time in the Word with brothers and sisters in Christ, applying the gospel truth to our hearts, which changes us by the power of the Holy Spirit.

- **When we serve**, we love one another by using our time, talents, and treasure, to make sure the gospel ministry continues in word and deed.

- **When we go**, we go out the doors of the church into our families, our communities, and to the world, proclaiming the Good News that sets people free and doing the good works that lead people to glorify God.

Here are some examples of people going out into the world doing good works. Do you see yourself in these examples?

- A teacher who pours himself into doing his work to the best of his ability, going the extra mile, not just to move a student to the next grade, but to instill a love for learning.

- The mom who makes school lunches, helps with science projects, and shows her children the love of Christ day after day.

- The person who quietly meets the need of the guard at their gatehouse.

- The retiree who uses his years of experience, financial resources, and business networks to advance the cause of a non-profit organization for Jesus's sake.

- The tenderhearted person who goes weekly to Pregnancy Resource Center to love and care for young girls and women in crisis.

- The family that intentionally gets involved in the life of their neighborhood—spending time in the yard in order to meet neighbors, inviting them to dinner, and bringing the blessing of Christ to their local community.

- The person who coaches a kids' sports team, helping athletes develop not only skills but also character as they model Christlikeness.

- The people who make a sacrificial offering as a faith promise pledge to support the spread of the gospel around the world.

- The person who volunteers to tutor people in our community so immigrants and others can learn to speak English.

- The person who "adopts" an elderly shut-in and makes a point to provide them with human contact and care on a regular basis.

- The person who goes week after week to local elementary schools and volunteers with Good News Club to care for children and share Jesus' love.

- The person who goes to St. Matthew's House to lead a Bible study for people struggling with addictions and homelessness.

- The person who spends a few hours each week just looking for ways to bless other people through random acts of kindness.

- The person who teams up with other believers to go into nursing homes in our community, to share the love of Jesus through hugs, smiles, and loving care.

The possibilities are endless. There's no limit to the good you can do each day or each week when you're *zealous* to do good works.

Go! Not because you must, not out of duty or because of an obligation to some law you feel imposed on you by God to pay him back for your salvation. No! Go under the reign and rule of God's grace and hope and love that has set you free to lavish love on the world around you.

I'm not calling you to add a bunch of new activities to your already busy calendar. This is a call to go about all those activities with a new sense of purpose, as a representative of Christ. This is about *you + a changed heart.* It's when God's grace, hope, and love give you the ability to see everything with fresh eyes—as an opportunity to do good works.

> **When the gospel grips your heart,**
> **you will increasingly become**
> **a person zealous to do good,**
> **wherever you are, whenever you can.**

This is my vision for us as a church. A people so captivated by the grace of the gospel, so inspired by the love of Christ as we **worship**, **grow**, and **serve**, that we can't wait to **go** into the world to proclaim the good news and do good works.

What good are you ready to do in Jesus's name?

BETWEEN YOU AND GOD

1. Do you believe in your heart that you do not need to earn God's favor and he loves you unconditionally? Talk to him about this, if it's hard to accept. Thank him that it's true, even if your heart isn't quite on board yet.

2. Do you do good works joyfully, out of gratitude for what Christ has done for you? Or do you serve out of duty, because you know you're "supposed" to serve? What would it take for serving to feel more like a gift to you than a burden?

3. What keeps you going when you feel "weary in well-doing?" Think about whether you are serving too much or too little and why. Ask God for help in finding the right balance.

---

[1] Jerry Bridges, *The Discipline of Grace: God's Role and Our Role in the Pursuit of Holiness* (NavPress, 1994), 85.
[2] Tim Chester, *Titus For You* (The Good Book Company, 2014), 77.
[3] N.T. Wright, *Surprised by Hope* (Harper One, 2008), 193.

Chapter 10

"BUT WHAT ABOUT..."

Have you ever read a book and thought afterward, "I wish I could ask the author a few questions like, 'What did you mean when you said this?' or 'How did you handle this issue in your *own* life?'" It's similar to conversations we've all had where you sit down with a friend to talk about something we've just read.

My collaborator on this book, Verla Wallace, is an experienced journalist and interviewer who asked me some of these kinds of questions. We decided to include them here, so you could be part of the conversation. In fact, I hope you will start your own conversation about discipleship with those around you, as we all seek to fulfill our high calling to be fully devoted followers of Christ.

*   *   *

VW: Why do you think discipleship sometimes feels so daunting?

TC: Maybe it's because we're not clear about what discipleship entails. At its heart, it's learning Christ—walking with him by faith, learning who he is and what it means to follow him day-to-day in loving obedience to the good news of the gospel. But that's sort of a vague concept until you put some "meat on the bone," to explain what it looks like in a practical way. That's the point of this book. It's not the whole story about discipleship, but it covers the main building blocks in the context of the local church. I'm hoping the book will demystify what it means to follow Christ.

A Personal Journey of Faith

*VW: Throughout the book, you come back again and again to the mandate given by God for every believer to share the gospel and be part of someone else's journey to find Christ. Who or what influenced **your** decision to accept Christ?*

TC: Well, my journey to faith was a slow one. I heard the gospel many times growing up in a church that faithfully taught the Word. And my parents had an enormous influence on me as I watched their faith and genuine devotion lived out day-to-day. As a young child I made numerous professions of faith starting at four years old and to the best of my young understanding, I wanted to be a Christian.

But like many people my understanding of the gospel and salvation was deeply flawed. I had no sense that God had ever *saved* me from anything. I somehow had the idea that "keeping" my salvation was dependent on me staying in God's good graces by my good behavior. I did not perceive God to be loving, but rather stern and eager to send me to hell if I didn't "walk the line." Not surprisingly, as I grew older, I became disillusioned about Christianity.

VW: Who or what brought you back to Christ?

TC: Ultimately it was God who drew me to himself. This is always the case, but we rarely see it until we're looking backward. In college, several different factors came together that caused me to begin re-examining Christianity. One factor God used was a Christian roommate who is still a good friend of mine. He was not a model Christian by any measure, as he himself would attest, but his relationship with God was real and we had many good conversations that were instrumental to me following Christ. Ultimately I ended up attending his church and became friends with his pastor, Andy Hawkins. To this day, Andy continues to be an important influence in my life, along with my childhood pastor Jack Bohman. Those three men all played a very significant role in my becoming a follower of Jesus.

Another major factor was meeting my wife Emily. She had made a faith commitment in middle school, but by the time we met, Christ wasn't central in her life. So this period was a real turning point in both our lives.

When we began to get serious as a couple and started talking about someday having a family and building a life together, I was fearful. We knew deep down inside that we needed something besides our own wisdom to achieve a healthy family and marriage. We needed a higher authority—something or someone we were both devoted to—to help us weather the storms of life. I credit my parents for instilling in me by example the importance of a Christ-centered marriage.

But, to be honest, at first, we started looking more closely at Christianity strictly as a practical means of getting what we wanted—a good marriage and a healthy family. As a first step toward that end, we decided to start reading the Bible and doing devotions together, long-distance. Emily was in college in another state at the time.

VW: So, while your seeking began as a practical, transactional, spiritual quest, what happened?

TC: I remember the shock of having all my distorted views of God totally dismantled by what God's Word actually *said*. I began to see a picture of God as someone who was full of grace, who genuinely *loved* people and loved *me,* someone who actually wanted to be compassionate and forgive my sins. That was a real turning point. As I continued the process of being in the Word with Emily and by myself, and talking with my roommate and going to church with him, my life began to change. The message of the gospel began to take root in my heart.

VW: Was there an "aha!" moment when you renewed your faith commitment as an adult or was it more of a gradual awakening?

TC: I remember one evening I was sitting at my desk in my apartment, reading in Lamentations 3, of all places. I had been under deep conviction for about a month that I had been a person who grew up *knowing* the truth but still rejecting it over and over. I was very depressed feeling I had sinned beyond God's willingness to extend me grace. It all came to a head that evening when I realized like I never had before that I was a sinner who justly deserved to go to hell and that God didn't *have* to save me if he didn't want to. It was a really sad but inescapable conclusion!

It was then that I was reading in Lamentations 3:16-18 which says, *"He has made my teeth grind on gravel, and made me cower in ashes; my soul is bereft of peace; I have forgotten what happiness is; so I say, 'My endurance has perished; so has my hope from the LORD.'"*

Even though the prophet Jeremiah spoke those words in a different context, it was the closest thing I'd ever felt to God speaking directly to me. The words perfectly expressed the condition of my heart. I had no peace, no happiness, because I knew I had spurned the only thing in life that mattered—a relationship with God. I was without hope.

But then I read the next few verses: *"Remember my affliction and my wanderings, the wormwood and the gall! My soul continually remembers it and is bowed down within me. But this I call to mind, and therefore I have hope: The steadfast love of the Lord never ceases; his mercies never come to an end; they are new every morning; great is your faithfulness. 'The Lord is my portion,' says my soul, 'therefore I will hope in him.'"*

These words also expressed what I felt in my heart. At that moment, I happened to be listening to one of my roommate's worship CD's. The song playing was, "Open the Eyes of My Heart, Lord." I closed my eyes and began to sing this song as my prayer and in that moment everything changed.

I went from despair and feeling no hope to knowing this is the only thing that matters. I remember thinking, "God has forgiven all my sins and he has genuinely taken my sins away, and now I have a *real* relationship with him. He loves me! I'm ready to live my life for him."

I laugh when I think about how I went into my Finance class that next day and sat down next to a guy and blurted out, "You know, God is really who he says he is and he loves you. He can take away your sins and give you a new start!" He looked at me kind of funny, because we had never had any conversation like that before. He probably thought I was a little crazy!

Discipleship: It's Messy.

VW: Was that moment of transformation when your own life of discipleship began?

TC: Yes, but it was not all smooth sailing from there. Growing up in a Christian home, I knew the importance of prayer, Bible reading, and sharing my faith with others, so I wanted to start doing all those things right away. But, in my immaturity, I became prideful and self-righteous about how zealously I practiced my faith. I thought, "If everyone else would start doing what *I'm* doing, God would feel as good about *them,* as he did me!" I felt God liked me before, but, because I was working so hard at being an over-achieving Christian, now he would *really* like me!

Even though I knew I was saved by grace, I still felt my ongoing walk with God was dependent on my performance. And God in his grace allowed me to have some stumbles in that season. I made some bad decisions that were devastating to me and I thought, "Now what? *Now,* where do I stand with God? Does he still love me if I'm not *good*?" I again began to despair. Clearly I knew the gospel was the means by which I entered the Christian life, but I did not yet know that believing the gospel is the key to every day in the Christian life.

VW: So the salvation issue was settled, but not the surrender part.

TC: Right. God brought me to a place where I realized I had messed up my life and was going to *keep* messing it up if I was in charge of it. It all came to a head one evening when I had to make some difficult decisions that I was afraid to make and do some things I was afraid to do, in terms of obeying him. I remember coming to a place where I knew I couldn't negotiate my way out of this. It had to be God's way and not my way.

"Alright, Lord," I said, "I'm scared to death of what this might mean. But if you can take my life and make something of it, it's yours. I'm all yours."

It was such a freeing thing! I felt like God could be trusted and I could put my whole life in his hands. That's why you'll hear me preach so often that you really *can* trust God with your whole life and do what he asks you to do. If the gospel is true, and it is, then we have nothing to fear by surrendering everything to him. There's no greater joy than to be fully surrendered to Christ.

Shortly after that time, Emily and I began to feel a call to the ministry. It came out of the blue. I felt I was growing as a

Christian, but vocational ministry had never crossed my mind because I didn't feel worthy, and Emily felt the same way. I knew my crooked heart, my pride, and my self-righteousness.

However, over time I began to understand not only how the gospel provides for our initial salvation, but also how it governs our everyday walk with God. None of it is about staying in God's good graces by our own efforts and discipleship. I'm already *in* God's good graces because of what Jesus has done. His invitation to me is to walk in it, live in it, enjoy it, and learn from him. All of my discipleship activities are a response to what he's already done and secured for me.

Discipleship: There's a Learning Curve

VW: The performance trap strikes all of us at some point. Our culture measures and rewards "doing." But there's another pitfall at the other end of the spectrum: where a person is a Christian but is spiritually stagnant and can't seem to muster the "want-to" to grow as a believer. They may say, "Hey, I'm not perfect, but I'm basically a decent person. I believe in God. I'm a good husband and provider. Our family attends church. I'm just not sure I want to get all that 'revved up' about Christianity."

TC: Good observation. There's no doubt that the desire and conviction to grow come from Christ. I spent many years where I had no desire for spiritual things, no "want-to."

VW: Does that mean we're "off the hook"—that if Jesus wants me to grow, he must do all the "heavy lifting"?

TC: No. We have a part to play. In our Reformed tradition, we talk about the "means of grace." They are things that don't *create* grace, but they open up the *flow* of grace in our lives and communicate to us the benefits of what Christ has accomplished for us. Spending time in the Word is one "means" of grace, particularly hearing the Word preached in the context of worship and celebrating the Lord's Supper. Spending time in prayer and fellowship with other believers is another means of grace. These are means God uses to create faith in us and to strengthen our faith in Christ's work on our behalf.

As we communicate with God in prayer we should be totally honest with him. Tell him that you don't have a strong desire to grow in your faith and you need his help to be hungrier. As I mentioned earlier in the book, a lot of times we don't recognize our spiritual hunger because we're filling our lives with so many distractions. We mask the hunger that's there by temporarily satiating ourselves with lesser things, but only he can satisfy. A good place to start is to take an honest self-inventory of your spiritual life. It may be that the gospel has short-circuited somewhere in your heart and that an idol has replaced Christ at the center.

VW: Distractions aren't the only issue. It's the speed and volume of the information that bombards us in print, over the airwaves, and on our electronic devices. Even important information is condensed into 45-second sound bites for a ravenous 24-hour news cycle. To deal with it all, our attention span gets shorter and shorter.

TC: Not only are we not willing to read an article that spells out an extended explanation of a subject, but our ability to *think deeply* for extended periods of time about something is also impaired.

VW: We've talked about discipleship-run-amok, where a person tries to earn points with God by their "performance" as a Christian. And we've talked about people at the other end, who *have little interest in spiritual growth. But what about the Christian who wants to grow, but—for whatever reason—their tank is empty. Even devoted Christians go through dry spells. What do **you** do to "refuel the tank" when you feel empty?*

TC: I do have times of dryness, like everybody else. I think the first thing a person must do is pay attention to their own patterns of behavior and what they're telling you. For example, when I find my cup is empty, it's almost always because I have something that needs to be dealt with personally or professionally or relationally and I'm avoiding it because I feel too empty to deal with it. That emptiness can affect how intentional I am about my spiritual disciplines. I don't want to talk to God about it. I don't want to open the Word. In other words, my dry spells don't have to do with my relationship with God as much as something else in my life that I don't want to address, such as a conflicted or tense relationship. And generally I'm not addressing it because I've forgotten some aspect of the gospel, such as the fact that I'm accepted in Christ and therefore need not fear owning my sin or being rejected by anyone. It's not the same for everyone, but that's a pattern I watch out for in myself.

VW: So what do you do about it?

TC: I have to deal with "the thing," whatever that "thing" is. That's when I go to God and say, "I'm feeling disconnected from you and I realize that (at least in this situation), this 'thing' is distracting me. I can't sit still and concentrate. I need to deal with this and I need your help to do so. Forgive me for not living in the freedom you purchased for me and help me now to walk in it."

VW: But sometimes a dry spell isn't so easily addressed. It turns into a real "wilderness" time. It may be precipitated by a health crisis or a divorce or you lose your job. You're praying your brains out but you don't see answers to your prayers or see God at work in your life (at least in a visible way). It feels like God has moved and left no forwarding address! Would you share one of those experiences in your own life and how you got through it?

TC: A number of years ago I found myself in the middle of a group of simultaneous circumstances that threw me into a pretty deep depression. In hindsight, I can see now how all the circumstances *brought* me to that place, but at the time I couldn't see it. It was exactly as you describe. I didn't understand what was happening and I couldn't seem to climb out of it.

I was seeing a Christian counselor at the time and ultimately ended up seeing a physician who prescribed medication for my clinical depression. I took the medication for about nine months, if I remember correctly. It was a helpful tool God used to enable me to address the underlying issues in my life, but it was a rough season. During that time I found I wasn't very interested in reading the Bible except for the Psalms. It was the only section of Scripture that I seemed to connect with. During wilderness times, sometimes you have no language for how you're feeling. I would pray the Psalms back to God and they became my voice. It was not a "way out" but a "way through."

VW: In contrast to those dark days, in the past few years where have you seen God work noticeable transformation in your life?

TC: Like all believers, I'm a work-in-progress. So for every area where I can see progress, I can see *other* areas that still await needed change. God is patient with me and I'm becoming increasingly patient with myself as well. But one area where I see real change is in the area of joy—what joy is, where it's found, what I have to do to cultivate joy. I'm a far more joyful person than I used to be. It started when I realized the connection between joy and gratitude. I find that when I intentionally cultivate an attitude of gratitude, joy rises.

Furthermore, there are three verses in 1 Thess. 5:16-18 that have become my daily marching orders. These verses are at the center of my own personal "rule of life" that Steve Macchia talks about in his book, *Crafting a Rule of Life: An Invitation to the Well-Ordered Way*: "**Rejoice** always, **pray** without ceasing, **give thanks** in all circumstances, for this is the will of God in Christ Jesus." [Emphasis added.]

Before I understood the power of those verses, I had the attitude, "If I feel joy, great. If not, bummer." Now I see these instructions as something for me to hold onto and live out by faith and the joy follows. When I'm in difficult circumstances, I say to myself, "Even now, by the grace I've received through Christ, God's will for me is joy, prayerfulness, thanksgiving. Therefore, I *will* rejoice, I'm going to *give* thanks, I'm going to pray *anyway*, even when things don't turn out as I planned. I'm going to thank God for all the *other* things I *can* be legitimately thankful for." In other words, if I don't feel joy, I am more intentional about stirring it up through prayer, thanksgiving, and faith in the good news.

Keeping Faith Strong

VW: Setting aside those difficult seasons we all occasionally encounter, let's talk about what is your routine for personal spiritual growth. On most days I assume you spend a certain amount of time on sermon preparation. That's part of your vocational work. What do you do differently when you're having personal devotions, to keep it different and fresh from all the other time you're spending in Scripture? Do you have a specific regimen you follow or do you mix it up?

TC: Some things stay the same and some things change. I love to get up early, so my normal pattern is to rise well before the sun. I know that's not for everyone, but I count it a gift from God that I actually enjoy it! Most of the time I try not to check email or online news sites or Facebook when I first get up. I find they just set my mind racing about various things that make it harder to be sensitive to what God is saying through his Word and prayer. Instead, while I wait for the coffee to brew, I usually read a chapter from a biography of some well-known Christian. Biographies are an easy start to the day and provide me with immediate inspiration and encouragement. Right now, I'm reading the biography of George Whitefield in very short increments.

With coffee in hand, I go upstairs to my study and get into the Word. I use different Bible reading plans at different times. For a long time, I was going through Scripture very slowly, spending multiple days in one chapter and extended time in the Psalms. But I felt it was time to step back and get a broader perspective for a while.

My recent Bible reading plan was reading from ten different chapters in the Bible a day. It's designed to give you a sense of the whole of Scripture. I've been doing it with two other guys and we get together once a week to talk about what we're reading and what God is teaching us through it. However, after a while I found that ten chapters a day, every day, became a little too much for this season. As of January 1, along with my family and our church family, I'm following the church Bible reading plan using the Read Scripture app and I'm loving it.

VW: It's like when you're on a plan to read the entire Bible in a year. You start out strong. Then you get the flu or take a vacation, you get a few days behind, and you're toast!

TC: Right. You start out strong and then it can reach a place where you're just trying to hammer out chapters without regard to doing what it says. That can happen with Bible reading plans. They start out helping you and sometimes become a burden. Don't get me wrong, I'm 100% in favor of Bible reading plans and I think everyone should have a plan for reading Scripture. In particular, I'm hopeful that many people at Covenant are thriving on the Read Scripture plan. But now I strive to maintain a balance—being intentional while at the same time being flexible. There's a place for discipline but there's also a place for recognizing our humanity. This has been another area of growth for me over the years as the implications of the gospel have seeped deeper into my heart.

VW: Do you journal?

TC: Yes, I do. As I'm reading, I'm asking the Lord, "What do you want to say to me today?" And, of course, I ask myself basic Bible study questions like, "What does this tell me about God? What does it show me about who I am? What's the main truth I should take away?" Then, I journal about my thoughts and observations.

I ask myself, "How would my life be different if I believed this was really true?" That's the question that really helps me apply Scripture to my life. If I really believe that God is in control, how would my life be different? If I really believe that Christ is present now to help me do what he's called me to do, how would I behave differently? That's usually a lead-in to a time of prayer.

VW: Do you have a particular system for prayer—like praying for family and related issues on Mondays, the church issues on Tuesday, our country and world on Wednesdays, and so on?

TC: There are lots of ways to do prayer and there's no *one* right way. For the last three years I've been using the prayer card system described in the book, *A Praying Life* by Paul E. Miller.

VW: How does it work? Do you have a separate card for every person or thing for which you're praying?

TC: I do. I have a stack of 3x5 index cards with scriptures and prayer requests for the important people and issues in my life. So I have different cards for Emily and each child. Over time, I add to what's on their card—things I want to see God do in their life, praying for things *they* want prayer for, praying for the kids' future spouses and so on.

Then, I have cards for different ministries in the church, different things in my own life, things happening in the world, people I want to see come to know Christ, people in the church who have asked for prayer, and so on. I don't get through all of them every day, but I keep cycling through them. One of the most exciting things is getting to write answers to those prayers on the cards and being reminded of them each time I cycle through.

VW: Is music part of your personal devotional time?

TC: I keep a hymnal by my desk and often quietly sing a song from it or meditate on the words of a hymn. Sometimes I'll go on YouTube and sing along with a more contemporary worship song that isn't in a traditional hymnal. Music is a helpful tool to assist us in worship.

VW: You've outlined a pretty ambitious daily devotional regimen. Do you think the average person is likely to spend that kind of time every day? Plus, there's the whole thing about personality types and how they affect the way we connect daily with God.

Some people are very disciplined left-brain folks like you, who like to have a plan and work the plan. They find it easy to follow a disciplined routine. Others, however, are more free-form types.

That may do an hour of heavy Bible reading one day and 15 minutes on a Bible app the next day...or prayer in the car on the way to work, maybe journaling over lunch, and 30 minutes of Bible study before bed. I've heard believers say, "I want to be consistent with my spiritual growth, but I don't have big chunks of available time. How much is 'enough?' How do I know if I'm getting it right?"

TC: There's no hard and fast prescription in the Bible. We know what the basic components should be—prayer, time in the Word, singing songs of praise, and other things we've discussed. And the time when you do it is up to the individual. It will look different for everyone. But whenever and however we do it, it's meant to be a daily time to remember who God is and who he isn't, a time of giving him praise and reverence, of listening and honoring and ultimately reapplying the truth of the gospel to our lives.

The bottom line is that while people have different temperaments, it's about setting aside *some* time every day for one purpose—to be with God.

Making Family Worship Work

VW: You talk in the book about family worship or devotions— how it doesn't have to be long and drawn out but it can be just a few verses, a song, a prayer, maybe a story. What do you do when a family has kids in a wide range of ages? For example, in a home with teenagers, it's not uncommon for them to leave the house at 7 in the morning and have after-school activities as well. It's a challenge to have a meal together, much less to have family devotions. Also, how do you structure family worship with kids of different ages and different levels of interest and intelligence?

TC: There are a couple things that may be helpful. First, not everyone has to be there for worship to happen. Of course, we *want* everybody there, but that may be unrealistic. At this point in our family's life, I'm the one most likely to be out and Emily does a great job of carrying it on without me.

Admittedly, it's a little easier in our family right now because we have young children. But, even at their age, there are nights when we're away from home or other circumstances interfere. However, when we're home, our practice is to sit down together in the living room, right before bedtime for devotions. For other people, maybe it's 10 minutes around the breakfast table, saying a brief prayer together. Sometimes before the kids go off to school while they're eating breakfast, we'll talk about some principles from Proverbs that will be helpful to remember as they go off to their work. Do whatever works for your family, but make *room* for it in your life. Emily does an amazing job of making sure we get through dinner and have the space to sit down and do this before bedtime.

As far as dealing with kids of different ages, it's important that whoever is leading the devotional time help each person in the group see how whatever is being said or read applies to them. Currently we're using the Read Scripture app as a family, and before that we were reading *Pilgrim's Progress*.

VW: Really? That's a tough book for young kids to understand, isn't it? All that archaic language is even hard for adults to understand!

TC: I wanted them to hear the richness of the language, though I do simplify a fair amount of it as we go. I think we parents sometimes set lower expectations for kids than they can actually handle. The book *is* a bit of a challenge, even for Emily and me, but it's working. We would read a small section and then talk about how it might apply to each of them. That's something you can do at any age. We've also been through *The Jesus Storybook Bible* and *The Big Picture Story Bible* many times each and found them very helpful, as well as some other books. Singing songs also can be done at any age. During our prayer time, sometimes Emily or I will pray for everyone, but other times I'll ask each person to pray for someone else in the group. The point is to have some things that are constant, like a regular time, but also some variety, so it doesn't get boring and is realistic to maintain.

VW: Talk a bit about what happens when the kids get older. Some families have teenagers who reach a stage where they're not interested in family devotions. Would you insist they participate because they are living under your roof or do you let them make their own decision?

TC: I'm not faced with that situation yet, so I can't speak from personal experience. But I would say, "If you're home, we expect you to join us. If you choose to be present but not participate, that's your choice, but this is family time. We at least want to know how we can be praying for you." Then we have to trust that the hearing of God's Word—even if someone is not participating—will be used by God to draw a person back to himself. I don't think it's unreasonable to set that expectation for those who live in your household.

In a Nutshell

*VW: What have you learned about the Christian life that you wish somebody had told you sooner...or that someone **did** tell you and you think others would benefit from knowing?*

TC: Hmmm. Interesting question. The first thing I wish I had learned earlier was that transformation happens largely in the context of *relationships* with others. Early on in my Christian life, I was under the impression that getting more knowledge was the answer to dealing with sin issues or besetting sins or attitudes or dispositions we get stuck in. I thought, "If I just read one more book or hear one more lecture about this, I'll know how to handle it." But now I have a Master of Divinity degree, a Doctor of Ministry degree, and I've read hundreds of books. What I've found is that knowledge is just knowledge. It's not unimportant, but apart from caring Christian relationships it's hard to make any progress in spiritual maturity.

Secondly, I've learned that the fundamental challenge of the Christian life isn't doing it. Rather, it is believing the gospel is what it says it is, that God is who he says he is, and I am who he says I am. Almost every issue I've had boils down, at some point, to believing (or not believing) that the gospel is true, that I'm really set free, and that if God is for me, who can stand against me? All my sins have been pardoned and I stand before God dressed in the righteousness of Christ (which is what justification means). Who can condemn me? What have I to fear?

VW: You're at the front end of your pastoral ministry. Do you ever think about the legacy you hope to leave someday? If you died tomorrow, how you would want to be remembered?

TC: It would not be something about myself, but about Jesus. The message I would want people to take from my life and my ministry is that Jesus is enough…for you, for me, for all of us.